The politics of everyday China

MANCHESTER
1824

Manchester University Press

POCKET POLITICS

SERIES EDITOR: BILL JONES

Pocket politics presents short, pithy summaries of complex topics on socio-political issues both in Britain and overseas. Academically sound, accessible and aimed at the interested general reader, the series will address a subject range including political ideas, economics, society, the machinery of government and international issues. Unusually, perhaps, authors are encouraged, should they choose, to offer their own conclusions rather than strive for mere academic objectivity. The series will provide stimulating intellectual access to the problems of the modern world in a user-friendly format.

Previously published
The Trump revolt   Edward Ashbee
Lobbying   Wyn Grant
Power in modern Russia   Andrew Monaghan
Reform of the House of Lords   Philip Norton
Government by referendum   Matt Qvortrup
Transatlantic traumas   Stanley R. Sloan

The politics of everyday China

Neil Collins and David O'Brien

Manchester University Press

Copyright © Neil Collins and David O'Brien 2019

The right of Neil Collins and David O'Brien to be identified as the authors of
this work has been asserted by them in accordance with the Copyright, Designs
and Patents Act 1988.

Published by Manchester University Press
Altrincham Street, Manchester M1 7JA
www.manchesteruniversitypress.co.uk

British Library Cataloguing-in-Publication Data
A catalogue record for this book is available from the British Library

ISBN 978 1 5261 3180 5 paperback

First published 2019

The publisher has no responsibility for the persistence or accuracy of URLs
for any external or third-party internet websites referred to in this book, and
does not guarantee that any content on such websites is, or will remain,
accurate or appropriate.

Typeset by Out of House Publishing
Printed in Great Britain
by CPI Group (UK) Ltd, Croydon, CR0 4YY

In memory of Denis
For Shani

Contents

Boxes

Preface

Each evening at sunset in Beijing's vast Tiananmen Square, soldiers of the People's Liberation Army (PLA; 人民解放军) march from the Forbidden City through the Gate of Tranquillity in perfect formation for the lowering of the national flag. It is an impressive sight of precision and power and always gathers a large crowd of tourists and other onlookers. This ceremony draws a direct line from the traditions of imperial China, taking place at what was the spiritual heart of the empire, to the birth of the People's Republic of China (PRC; 中华人民共和国), announced on this spot by Mao Zedong (毛泽东) in October 1949. From an enormous portrait on the gate, Chairman Mao still gazes down on the ceremony, flanked on either side by the slogans 'Long Live the People's Republic of China' and 'Long Live the Great Unity of the World's Peoples'. Other slogans nearby celebrate current Party and State leader Xi Jinping's (习近平) 'Chinese Dream of National Rejuvenation'. As the soldiers carefully lower the flag, standing among the crowd are numerous tall young men in smart white shirts and black slacks carrying large black, folded umbrellas. These are plainclothes security officers, and their job is to watch for any possible disturbance. The umbrellas are to shield any such unpleasantness while protestors are whisked away. The security men also have a fire extinguisher by their feet in case of self-immolation from monks or other demonstrators, which has occurred in Tibet and other areas of China. This is, after all, the sight of student protests in 1989 which almost brought the Chinese Communist Party (CCP) to its knees.

This combination of an ostentatious celebration of the power of tradition with such anxiety is perhaps symbolic of where the PRC is today. On the one hand, it is more prosperous, more stable, more confident and more peaceful than it has been at any time in the past 200 years, possibly ever. There remains however a grave apprehension for the authorities that disorder and chaos are close by and that the hard-won harmony (和谐) and civilisation (文明) are under threat. President Xi has repeatedly stressed the importance of reading Confucius (孔子) for today's Chinese, in a marked difference from his predecessor Mao who wanted all trace of Confucius eliminated. In the Confucian tradition, a leader must above all else ensure order and stability. If he fails and chaos breaks out, the 'mandate of heaven' (天命) will be removed and the empire will fall. Xi, China's most powerful leader since Mao, is determined to not let that happen.

Abbreviations

BRI	Belt and Road Initiative
CCDI	Central Commission for Discipline Inspection
CCP	Chinese Communist Party
CMC	Central Military Commission
NPC	National Party Congress
PLA	People's Liberation Army
PRC	People's Republic of China
SOE	State-owned enterprise
VPN	Virtual Private Network

Introduction

THE economic, diplomatic and technological achievements of China, when compared to those of other countries and regions, have long been the focus of intense scrutiny and speculation, yet accounts of the political changes that underlie China's recent remarkable story vary greatly in their concentration. Some try to identify long-standing historical patterns dating to the earliest dynasties and before. Other more contemporary studies emphasise the geopolitical elements that underpin China's rise. A common theme is the relative strength and durability of the political models of governance offered by an authoritarian China versus the liberal democracies of the West. In this book, however, the aim is to provide the reader with insights into ways in which politics affects the everyday lives of Chinese people. This is not to understate the impact of political culture – the deeply embedded distinctive patterns of political, economic and social behaviour that fundamentally shape politics. Indeed, the critical difference in the reaction of Chinese citizens, compared with other people, to superficially similar innovations and events can only be fully understood with reference to such cultural distinctiveness.

This book looks at how the contract between the Chinese state and its citizens produces compliance and apparent support despite the problems of corruption, food scandals, air pollution and the constraints on personal freedom. It explores how China's past is presented as both a mandate for a party-political monopoly and a promise of a glorious future. It does so through the voice of China's people, by exploring the lived experiences of her citizens across a wide range of socio-economic, rural, urban, ethnic and religious backgrounds.

Though frequently portrayed and indeed depicting itself as a homogenous monolith, the PRC is full of contradictory and fascinating complexity. From its multi-ethnic population of hugely varied languages, races and religions to its contrasting landscapes of futuristic mega-cities and rural poverty, it is a land of enormously diverse people and places. *The Politics of Everyday China* explores some of the critical issues from the perspectives of the newly prosperous middle classes, ever more pressurised by skyrocketing house prices and living costs, and of farmers and workers once idealised in revolutionary propaganda, who feel increasingly marginalised. From the ideologies of Marxism-Leninism and Mao Zedong that are taught by the ruling Communist Party to the ultra-consumerism of its shopping centres and millionaires, China is a nation of sometimes uncomfortably coexisting ideas and narratives.

Of course, behind the routine experience of growing up, studying, working and raising a family in China is the influential framework of ideology, material conditions and geopolitical considerations. Chinese politics is shaped by deeply held beliefs and attitudes that, though not fixed forever, change slowly even in the face of marked discontinuities in the institutional arrangements of the State. Similarly, the context of everyday lives includes the 'events' of which Harold Macmillan, the British prime minister, is said to have warned. For example, one day in mid-January 2018, the morning news began with the arrest of Gen. Fang Fenghui (房峰辉), a former PLA Chief of Joint Staff and a member of the Central Military Commission.[1] For the listeners, this report only made sense in the context of the crackdown initiated by Xi Jinping, who became president in 2012, ushering in a major push to rid China of corruption. Back in 2007, then President Hu Jintao (胡锦涛) warned: 'Resolutely punishing and effectively preventing corruption bears on the public's support for the Party and its very survival, and is, therefore, a primary political task the Party must attend to at all times.'[2]

His successor has taken this advice to heart and is just as conscious of the need for the ruling CCP to secure the ready support of ordinary Chinese citizens.

In late 2017, Chinese citizens shared the disquiet of those elsewhere in Asia at the latest missile test by the Democratic People's Republic of Korea (North Korea), which they learned puts their neighbour close to having a real nuclear capability and threatening a global war. As with all mainstream news, the story stuck closely to the Beijing government's line. In this case, it was an expression of 'grave concern', but the Chinese observer is also able to place the event in a much longer account of China's role in the world – its dynastic past, nineteenth-century travails and the current revival of fortune.

For many, possibly the majority of Chinese citizens, the idea that there is something inevitable in the logic of history to suggest that their political system is a temporary step on the path to a Western version of democracy is just imperialism in another form. The phenomenal success of the Chinese economy is evidence enough for them that improved material conditions for everyday life do not require accessible choice at a political level. For the most part, the government of China, while not averse to resolute enforcement of its will, enjoys ready compliance with its policies and acquiescence to its authority. Indeed, its use of censorship and discouragement of an open debate may be seen by Chinese people as fulfilling the State's duty of care. Similarly, poor people, whose lives may be disrupted by urban renewal projects and similar schemes, often accept the disruption on the basis that the government is doing its best. In any event, the everyday logic of loyalty, as Hirschman would suggest, may be more compelling than either voice or exit.[3]

Yet President Xi Jinping has also presided over a clampdown on civil society and a purge of top leaders unprecedented since the Cultural Revolution. Numerous civil rights lawyers and activists have been detained, with many receiving long prison sentences, some of the most influential men in China have been brought before the courts and the internal security budgets have soared. The China of Xi Jinping is prosperous and peaceful, but it is also a place where those who challenge authority pay a heavy price and where resentment of stunning inequality abounds.

China has the world's largest population (1.4 billion) and exhibits a level of cultural and ethnic diversity present in few other countries. Its everyday politics reflects many of the cleavages found in other political systems. Urban and rural dwellers, the affluent and the poor, as well as the different generations, look to the government to meet competing demands. In China, the face of the State is often a local bureaucracy, and the workings of Beijing can seem remote. Decentralisation has encouraged local officials to compete in the promotion of economic development, but it has also slowed national programmes of reform. At times, the unethical behaviour of local bureaucrats does lead to open protest but, as with most of the imperial dynasties, the central regime enjoys legitimacy based on paternalistic characteristics that meld with Chinese culture.

The CCP is a monopoly party that can allocate public goods without challenge or the prospect of being removed from office. It nevertheless shares with commercial monopolies a need to retain the support of its customer base. In part, as this book discusses, it does this by attending to the everyday material and ideological needs and desires of the people. Among the goals it has declared central to its mission is returning China to its rightful place in the global order. The impediment to this is often portrayed as the pernicious influence of the West. Thus, for example, while others may see the conflict in the South China Sea as expansionist, the CCP presents China as a peace-loving country merely asserting its rightful historical claims against international conventions and laws purposely designed to serve Western interests. Similar assertions are found in the Party's account of its developmental role in Tibet and its rightful claims to Taiwan. On these issues, the proposition that the Party's monopoly is preserved in the interests of the people is seldom, if ever, challenged. Nationalistic and patriotic sentiments are easily aroused and, ironically, the CCP's task is sometimes to control them. The CCP has decided to fan the flames of this powerful nationalism to shore up its legitimacy, but the inherent dangers that exist with appealing to such emotions are apparent both nationally and internationally.

The Party is disciplined but not homogeneous. As in any political system, ideas about policy compete for implementation, and the priority given to addressing issues reflects the diverse interests of a vast country. As this book explores, social cleavages such as class, ethnicity and employment status make compromises inevitable. Some CCP members and officials have shown themselves to be particularly adept at promoting their views. Nevertheless, the appearance of unity is a priority, and new ideas must be seen to represent either continuity or sanctioned change. It is above all a unity behind Party General Secretary and President Xi Jinping who, in November 2017, at the five-yearly National Party Congress (NPC), saw his status as the most powerful Chinese leader since Chairman Mao confirmed.

The available scholarship on Chinese politics is enormous and an immense resource. This book draws from this abundant well but seeks to augment its explanation of the everyday politics of China with ethnographic material drawn from the authors' experience. The voices heard in this book are from Chinese people from across the country, from across social classes and backgrounds. Of course, the views expressed cannot be taken as representative of all; they are anecdotes, views and opinions which may be shared by many or by a few, but they are voices of real people who call China home. They have witnessed perhaps the most extraordinary transformation of any country in modern time. It is through these views that we attempt to illustrate in this short book how political decisions and polices actually impact upon people's daily lives. China is not a country where people can speak freely to researchers, especially foreign ones. All of the names used in this book are pseudonyms and descriptions are kept deliberately vague so as not to identify any informants. China today is stronger and more confident than at any time in the past century. It is, however, also a place of risk and fear where the reach of the Party extends into the private sphere and where those who are seen to cross or undermine authority suffer greatly.

Notes

1   D. Tse, 'Why General Fang Fenghui was purged', *The Diplomat* (14 January 2018), https://thediplomat.com/2018/01/why-general-fang-fenghui-was-purged/ (last accessed 14 May 2018).

2   'Full text of Hu Jintao's report at 17th Party Congress', *China Daily* (7 September 2010), www.chinadaily.com.cn/china/19th cpcnationalcongress/2010–09/07/content_29578561_8.htm (last accessed 14 May 2018).

3   A. O. Hirschman, *Exit, Voice, and Loyalty: Responses to Decline in Firms, Organizations, and States* (Boston, MA: Harvard University Press, 1970).

1

'It doesn't matter if the cat is black or white as long as it catches the mouse': the role of ideology in Communist China

ON a bright and freezing cold Saturday morning in Qingcheng Park (请城公园) in the centre of Hohhot, the provincial capital of the Inner Mongolia Autonomous Region, a crowd of roughly sixty pensioners has gathered for communal singing. Laughing and smiling and shuffling both in time with the music and to keep themselves warm in the icy temperatures, they belt out old revolutionary classics like 'Osmanthus Flowers Blooming Everywhere in August' and 'The East is Red'. This communal singing is fun, boisterous and clearly pleasantly nostalgic for the participants, but it also has a more profound relevance and meaning to the participants, as sixty-six-year-old Mr Wang, one of the singers, explains:

> We come here every Saturday even when it is very cold. It is always good to see friends and to sing the songs that we enjoy and remember from when we were younger. Most of the people you see here came to Hohhot a long time ago; they came to develop the borderlands and believed that they were doing the work of the Party, following the orders of Chairman Mao. We are proud of what we did then. It was tough. Hohhot was not like it is now with comfortable buildings and shops; back when I came here it was very poor. Life was very difficult, but now I live in great comfort. These songs are not just about the past. They are about showing our loyalty and our support for the Party and our gratitude for what it has done for us.

There is an almost religious aspect to it, although the participants would probably be horrified by such a comparison. Talking to the singers, one is struck not just by their energy and good humour but also by their faith. This is not some empty nostalgia or harking back to the old days, this seems more a celebration of their beliefs. Yet it is a celebration of an ideology which seems so utterly contradictory to the hyper-consumerism of today's China. Just outside the park gates are shopping malls and designer stores, while expensive cars clog the streets in Hohhot's terrible traffic jams. It all seems so paradoxical; how can China celebrate such overt capitalism and yet remain so loyal to the ideology of socialism?

'No CCP, no New China'

The CCP puts enormous efforts into crafting its ideological message and this is testified by the network of Party Schools across the country where officials are trained in ideological work.[1] This is much more than paying lip-service – cadres in China must engage in this type of training throughout their careers and must be able to show that they clearly understand the ideological line. These Party Schools are hugely influential and powerful in China, serving not only as centres for cadre training but also, in the words of Holbig, as a 'networking mechanism to enhance the chances of obtaining a higher office and a locus of a "cult of elitism"[2] from which the charisma of the Party emanates but also as a cradle for the ongoing innovation of Party theory'.[3]

The CCP had a total of approximately 89.5 million members at the end of 2016. Its membership increased by 688,000 from 2015, up 0.8 per cent. Of those, 23 million are women, accounting for just 25.7 per cent of the total membership, while 6.3 million members are from ethnic minority groups, making up 7 per cent of total membership.[4] Chairman Mao famously said that 'women hold up half the sky', yet in today's China they hold up just a quarter of the Party. They are also significantly underrepresented at the top of the leadership pyramid. No woman has ever been

Box 1.1   Joining the Party

'Jordan' Wang, a twenty-six-year-old postgraduate student who takes his English name from US basketball player Michael Jordan, was recently accepted into the Party.

'The whole process takes so long', he says, 'we have to pass difficult exams on Marxism and the history of the CCP. There is so much to study for this and it is really difficult. You must use the correct terminology and there is so much to remember'.

They also interview your classmates, teachers, people who know you, even my girlfriend, to make sure that you are a good person and will be a good fit. It is very strict; my friend was turned down because he gambles too much. They found out from interviewing his classmates.

They also look at your exam results and what organisations you have been involved in, sport, volunteering that sort of thing. Then there is a very tough interview, and finally, I was accepted.

My family was very proud. Both my father and my grandfather are members, and now I join them. It will be beneficial for my career, of course, but also, I do love the Party. It is the guiding light of our China, and by being a member, I will serve the people to continue its development.

I think of the Communist Party as being like my family. My mother and father supported me and love me and do all they can for me. The Party is also like this and now that I am an adult, like with my parents, I have responsibilities to look after them and to serve them. All the Chinese people think of the Party as being their family.

a member of the Standing Committee of the Politburo, the most powerful body in China, while they rarely make up more than one or two members of the Politburo, the next level down.[5]

To become a Party member is to join the Chinese elite. Potential members must pass many tests and demonstrate political correctness, moral integrity and, as Holbig puts it, 'spiritual loftiness through the skilful use of formal language' (see Box 1.1). Joining is only the first step, to advance a cadre must demonstrate their familiarity with ideology by putting it correctly into practice.[6] To the outsider, the term 'socialist' may seem an empty signifier, but inside the fold, it is vital to demonstrate adherence to and deep understanding of 'Socialism with Chinese Characteristics'.

In Xi Jinping's China, ideology is perhaps more critical now than at any time since the ideological campaigns of the 1960s and 1970s. 'We must uphold Marxism, firm up and further build the ideal of Communism and a shared ideal of socialism with Chinese characteristics, and nurture and practise core socialist values', Xi told the opening of the 19th NPC in November 2017. It is a prevalent theme for Xi. As Wang has shown in his analysis of ideology in President Xi's discourses, Xi frames the CCP's political ideologies as moral values with an authoritative nature that guides both the State and society, values that are at once stable but also are continually being adapted and Sinicised.[7] The ever-present double-negative propaganda slogan, 'No CCP, No New China' (没有共产党就没有新中国), succulently proclaims the Party's role.

The 2017 Congress saw 'Xi Jinping Thought on Socialism with Chinese Characteristics for a New Era' enshrined as a guiding principle of the Communist Party. This put Xi alongside only Chairman Mao in terms of his impact on Party ideology and ahead of his predecessors Hu Jintao, Jiang Zemin (江泽民) and Deng Xiaoping (邓小平), whose ideological teachings were never granted the term 'thought', only being referred to as 'theories'. For Yu Zhengsheng (俞正声), one of China's top leaders, Xi Jinping's Thought 'represents the latest achievement in adapting Marxism to the Chinese context, and is an important component of the system of theories of socialism with Chinese characteristics'. While for fellow Standing Committee member Zhang Dejiang (张德江), '[t]he Thought is the biggest highlight of the 19th National Congress of the Communist Party of China and a historic contribution to the Party's development'.[8]

Ideology and legitimacy

For Michael Freeden, ideology is a 'wide-ranging structural arrangement that attributes decontested meaning to a range of mutually defining political concepts'.[9] Where there is competition between ideologies, this competition is conducted largely over the control of political language. In China, the CCP has almost total control over political language. However, that does not mean that competition does not take place within the Party. As Holbig points out:

> In the authoritarian context of Communist one-party regimes, this competition is highly restricted as the Party claims hegemony in the ideological realm. Nevertheless, the (re)production of Party ideology remains a highly fluid framing process, where Marxist-Leninist and other traditional tenets of socialist ideology are constantly recombined with new political concepts such as nationalism, populism, the revitalisation of traditional culture etc.[10]

The oft-quoted Deng Xiaoping maxim, 黑猫白猫，能捉到老鼠就是好 ('it doesn't matter if the cat is white or black as long as it catches the mouse'), is often given as an example of his and China's subsequent ideological pragmatism which followed the end of the Mao era in 1976. The legitimacy of the CCP has, since Deng, become dependent on its ability to deliver economic progress and the assertion that China could modernise only under a strong one-party system.[11] Yet political ideology is also driven by the need for all political forces to legitimise their strategies and programmes by creating an appropriate intellectual narrative; it is this 'story' that is needed to justify their dominance.[12] In Xi

Jinping's China, in which the Party plays the central role in all aspects of political life, ensuring political legitimacy is the crucial task. While to outside observers China's leaders may pay only lip-service to socialism, in reality, adhering to this ideology is vital to ensure their legitimacy and survival. For the CCP, socialism provides the normative justification for the rightful source of political authority.[13]

Steve Tsang has put forward the concept of 'consultative Leninism' to describe the political system that has taken shape in China since the death of Deng Xiaoping. Consultative Leninism, he argues, has five defining characteristics: an obsessive focus on staying in power; continuous governance reform designed to pre-empt public demands for democratisation; sustained efforts to enhance the Party's capacity to elicit, respond to and direct changing public opinion; pragmatism in economic and financial management; and the promotion of nationalism in place of communism.[14] Under Xi Jinping, there has been a noticeable increase in the Party's activities in all of these areas. Ideology is its weapon in this vital battle and those who end up on the losing side face ruin.

Tigers and flies

One of the defining features of Xi Jinping's period in office has been a massive anti-corruption campaign. Shortly after taking power, Xi vowed to crack down on both 'tigers' and 'flies' – powerful leaders and lowly bureaucrats – in his campaign against graft. 'We must uphold the fighting of tigers and flies at the same time, resolutely investigating law-breaking cases of leading officials and also earnestly resolving the unhealthy tendencies and corruption problems which happen all around people', Xi said in a speech in January 2013.[15] This campaign has shown no sign of easing off as President Xi enters his second term in office. According to the Central Commission for Discipline Inspection (CCDI) of the CCP, authorities have registered about 1.16 million cases and taken disciplinary action against

1.2 million people. Under what the CCDI calls 'intense pressure', 57,000 Party members 'voluntarily' confessed to wrongdoings in 2016 alone. The numbers include 240 'tigers' and 1.14 million 'flies'. Discipline inspectors themselves are not immune. About 7,900 of them have been subject to disciplinary actions since 2012, according to the CCDI figures.[16]

The campaign has seen some of the most influential men in China imprisoned, from leading Standing Committee member Zhou Yongkang (周永康), who was sentenced to life in prison for taking 130 million yuan in kickbacks, to one of China's top generals, Xu Caihou (徐才厚), who died of bladder cancer after admitting to taking huge bribes. Xu was reported to have had one tonne of cash (US dollars, euros and renminbi) in the basement of his 21,500-square-foot Beijing mansion, as well as jade, emeralds, calligraphy and paintings.[17] Not since the Cultural Revolution have such high-ranking figures, and in such numbers, been purged.

One of the most astonishing falls from power was Bo Xilai (薄熙来), who back in 2012 had been tipped for elevation to the Standing Committee. Bo – a hugely charismatic Party Secretary of one of China's largest cities Chongqing – was best known nationally for his two campaigns, 'smashing black', which took on and eventually defeated Chongqing's notorious mafia, and 'singing red', a campaign to encourage residents in communal singing of revolutionary songs. Bo was seen as a leader of the leftist branch of the Party, which was calling for a return to a more Maoist position, who believed that economic and social reforms had gone too far. In the run-up to the important 18th NPC, which saw Xi elected Party General Secretary, Bo's faction was believed to be attempting to seize control of the top offices in the Party. Indeed, it was at the Congress that the accusations against Bo and his family were made public. His subsequent trial, along with that of his wife Gu Kailai (谷开来) who was convicted of the murder of English businessman Neil Heywood, transfixed the Chinese public. He was eventually found guilty of accepting bribes worth 20.44 million yuan and sentenced to life in prison.[18]

While the anti-corruption campaign has proven popular with a population who have long chafed against China's rampant graft, for Party cadres there is a real fear that they may be next in the firing line and that their safety depends on factors beyond their control. Mr Li, a forty-two-year-old official in the transportation bureau of a small east coast city, said:

> We live with this pressure every day; it is very stressful. Everybody is worried that their section will be investigated. If the inspectors come they go so deep and question everything. I do not believe I have done anything wrong but the way things work, it can be taken out of context, something made to look terrible. It is all about politics, all of the investigations are related to networks. It is a constant source of anxiety, and we do not know how this will all end. It makes sure people are very, very careful and very, very loyal. If you are seen to put your head up, they will bite it off.

Ideology in the classroom

For the CCP, adaptation is key to its political and ideological mission. One of the Party's self-described greatest strengths is its adaptability and innovation in promoting China's self-interest. This flexibility is central to the idea of Socialism with Chinese Characteristics. Holbig argues that the key to the ongoing legitimation of Party rule is 'the Party's skill in redefining [its] historical mission, creating a moving target that is always sufficiently far away to justify the CCP's long-term monopoly on leadership'.[19] It is this adaptability that allows Xi Jinping to stress the role of the market in the redistribution of resources while at the same time warning that any 'drifting away from or betraying Marxism will lead to the Party's losing its soul and direction as it moves forward'.[20]

As a keen student of history who will have given much thought to the student protests that culminated in the 1989 Tiananmen massacre, President Xi places particular importance on the role of ideological education in schools and universities and has called for improvements to be made to the ideological education classes that are mandatory for all Chinese students. He has stated 'that the goal of colleges and universities should be consistent with the whole country's development target and that their work should serve the people, the Party's governance, the development of the socialist system with Chinese characteristics and reform and opening-up, as well as the socialist modernisation drive'.[21] He also says that ideological work in colleges should be integrated into the entire education process, underlining the need for firm Party leadership in higher education. 'China's higher education institutions are under the leadership of the CCP, and are socialist colleges with Chinese characteristics, so higher education must be guided by Marxism, and the Party's policies in education must be fully carried out', he said in a 2016 speech.[22] The ideal of academic freedom so cherished in Western academic discourses just does not exist in China. The very idea of academic freedom is, in fact, anathema to the mission of the Communist Party.

In the view of the CCP, students' intellectual, ideological, emotional and psychological makeup has not matured, and they need guidance on where to channel their efforts in life, whom to love, how to appreciate things and what kind of person to be. In a 2016 essay, education minister Chen Baosheng (陈宝生) wrote that schools were the main target of hostile foreign forces that seek to infiltrate the country, while also complaining of 'historic nihilism' – code for attempts to question the Communist Party's rewriting of history. 'There are intense battles being fought at our education front line now', he said.[23]

When asked about ideological education classes in China, a standard response among students is that they are boring and not relevant. Xiao Wen, a twenty-two-year-old engineering student, is typical: 'We have to go to these classes once a week but truthfully none of my classmates take them seriously. The classes are so boring and the students are not even listening, just looking at their phones or day-dreaming. I don't think this is relevant to my life – it is boring and not what I am interested in. But we have to go so there is nothing we can do.'

Whose dream is it anyway?

Since Xi Jinping's rise to power in 2012, his reign has been perhaps defined by one slogan: 'The Chinese Dream' (中国梦). In the propaganda terms so common in China today this is 'the dream of all Chinese people to build a moderately prosperous society and realize national rejuvenation'. It has, of course, obvious echoes of the American Dream that has so defined the post-war American political and social experience, but it also has a particular resonance in a country that sees itself as having been humiliated by foreign powers for over a century. It is only the CCP which can overcome this humiliation and ensure it never happens again. Officially, the 'Chinese Dream' is the collective vision to achieve the 'Two 100s': first, the material goal of China becoming a 'moderately well-off society' by about 2020, around the CCP's 100th anniversary (2021); second, the modernisation goal of China becoming a fully developed nation by about 2050, around New China's 100th anniversary (2049) and it is only through Marxism that these dreams can be achieved.

The Party Constitution states the following:

> The Communist Party of China ... promotes core socialist values, adheres to Marxism as its guiding ideology, fosters the common ideal of socialism with Chinese characteristics, promotes patriotism-centred national spirit and the spirit of the times centring on reform and innovation and advocates the socialist maxims of honour and disgrace. It works to enhance the people's sense of national dignity, self-confidence and self-reliance, resist corrosion by decadent capitalist and feudal ideas and wipe out all social evils so that the people will have high ideals, moral integrity, a good education and a strong sense of discipline. It also needs to imbue its members with the lofty ideal of communism. The Party strives to develop

educational, scientific and cultural programs, carry forward the fine traditional culture of the Chinese nation, and develop a thriving socialist culture.

It is this understanding that allows the Party to see itself as the 'missing link' between the past and the future and the broker between 'traditional' and 'advanced' culture.[24] Under Xi Jinping, there has been an increasing emphasis on the CCP as the natural successor of traditional Chinese rule. 'The Chinese Communist Party is the successor to and promoter of fine traditional Chinese culture', Xi said in 2014.[25] The idea that the Party legitimacy comes not only from its position as the vanguard of the people but also from a Confucian idea of proper authority preventing chaos has strong resonance in China today. Combined with a more strident nationalism this is a powerful ideological mix but also a potentially combustible one.

The inherent contradictions were obvious in a campaign to clear illegal migrant worker residential areas of Beijing before the 19th NPC. The rate of the campaign was significantly increased after a horrific fire claimed the lives of nineteen workers, most of whom had come to Beijing seeking work. These migrant workers, who come from poorer provinces to build the capital's shopping malls and office towers, clean the homes of the wealthy and wait on tables in fine restaurants, have been described in official media and government publications as 'low-end population'. The term 'low-end population' seems to have surfaced in State media around 2010 to refer to those who work in low-end service jobs, including many that power China's digital economy giants,[26] or manufacturing. More recently, local officials from Beijing's districts have picked up on the phrase in official documents about restrictions on migration under a bigger plan to cap Beijing's population at twenty-three million by 2020.[27] Where these people fit within the Chinese Dream and how the CCP will react ideologically to conflict between the classes are some of the more sobering questions for the CCP as it nears the 100th anniversary of its foundation.

Among the generation who have known only double-digit economic growth rates, one is often struck by the lack of any interest in politics. This generation knows nothing of the chaos of revolution and seems to care even less, despite or perhaps because of all the ideological classes and propaganda. This apathy may suit the Party just fine for now, but it remains to be seen if, should economic growth decline significantly, the Socialism with Chinese Characteristics ideology has the strength to bear the weight.

Notes

1   K. Brown, 'The Communist Party of China and ideology', *China: An International Journal*, 10:2 (2012), 52–68.

2   F. Pieke, *The Good Communist: Elite Training and State Building in Today's China* (Cambridge: Cambridge University Press, 2009), 14–18.

3   H. Holbig, 'Ideology after the end of ideology: China and the quest for autocratic legitimation', *Democratization*, 20:1 (2013), 61–81.

4   Xinhua, 'CPC has nearly 89.5 mln members', *China Daily* (30 June 2016), http://usa.chinadaily.com.cn/china/2017–06/30/content_29952372.htm (last accessed 14 May 2018).

5   *Ibid.*

6   Holbig, 'Ideology after the end of ideology'.

7   J. Wang, 'Representations of the Chinese Communist Party's political ideologies in President Xi Jinping's discourse', *Discourse & Society*, 28:4 (2017), 413–35, p. 430.

8   *Ibid.*

9   M. Freeden, *Ideology: A Very Short Introduction* (Oxford: Oxford University Press, 2003), 54–5.

10 Holbig, 'Ideology after the end of ideology', p. 70.

11 M. Pei, *China's Crony Capitalism* (Cambridge, MA: Harvard University Press, 2016).

12 Brown, 'The Communist Party of China and ideology'.

13 Holbig, 'Ideology after the end of ideology'.

14 S. Tsang, 'Consultative Leninism: China's new political frame-work', *Journal of Contemporary China*, 18:62 (2009), 865–80.

15 T. Branigan, 'Xi Jinping vows to fight "tigers" and "flies" in anti-corruption drive', *Guardian* (22 January 2013), www.theguardian.com/world/2013/jan/22/xi-jinping-tigers-flies-corruption (last accessed 14 May 2018).

16 Y. Yang, 'Factbox: Seven facts of China's anti-corruption cam-paign', *Xinhua* (4 July 2017), http://news.xinhuanet.com/eng-lish/2017–07/04/c_136416939.htm (last accessed 14 May 2018).

17 A. Olesen, 'China reacts to massive corruption tally of a fallen general', *Foreign Policy* (22 November 2014), http://foreignpolicy.com/2014/11/22/china-reacts-to-massive-corruption-tally-of-a-fallen-general/ (last accessed 14 May 2018).

18 Xinhua, 'Bo Xilai gets life in prison', *China Daily* (22 September 2013), http://usa.chinadaily.com.cn/china/2013–09/22/content_16984347.htm (last accessed 14 May 2018).

19 Holbig, 'Ideology after the end of ideology'.

20 Y. Zhang, 'Adapting Marxism called crucial', *China Daily* (30 September 2017), www.chinadaily.com.cn/china/2017–09/30/content_32668217.htm (last accessed 14 May 2018).

21 X. Zhao, *China Daily* (9 December 2016), www.chinadaily.com.cn/china/2016–12/09/content_27617484.htm (last accessed 14 May 2018).

22 Xinhua, 'Xi calls for strengthened ideological work in colleges', *China Radio International* (9 December 2016), http://english.cri.cn/12394/2016/12/09/3521s946891.htm (last accessed 14 May 2018).

23 S. Denyer, 'China's president takes campaign for ideological purity into universities, schools', *Washington Post* (12 December 2016), www.washingtonpost.com/world/chinas-president-takes-campaign-for-ideological-purity-into-universities-schools/2016/12/12/2395ec42-c047–11e6-b20d-3075b273feeb_story.html (last accessed 14 May 2018).

24 Holbig, 'Ideology after the end of ideology'.

25 K. Jin, 'The Chinese Communist Party's Confucian revival', *The Diplomat* (30 September 2014), https://thediplomat.com/2014/09/the-chinese-communist-pa (last accessed 14 May 2018).

26 J. Horwitz, 'Beijing is evicting its migrants and displacing its e-commerce couriers', *Quartz* (27 November 2017), https://qz.com/1138278/beijing-is-evicting-its-migrants-and-displacing-its-e-commerce-couriers-who-work-for-companies-like-alibaba-and-jd/ (last accessed 14 May 2018).

27 Z. Huang, 'What you need to know about Beijing's crackdown on its "low-end population"', *Quartz* (22 November 2017), https://qz.com/1138395/low-end-population-what-you-need-to-know-about-chinas-crackdown-on-migrant-workers/ (last accessed 14 May 2018).

2

The road to revival

SINCE the Treaty of Westphalia in 1648, the idea of nation-states, as autonomous actors on the international scene with unquestioned authority within a clearly defined territory, has become the dominant unit of analysis for popular discussions of international relations. Indeed, rhetorically, almost all countries, regardless of size and strength, agree to respect each other's autonomy. In terms of self-image, however, China, which in Chinese is 中国 (*Zhong Guo*) – literally, the Middle Country – is not just another nation-state in the Westphalian sense but a 'civilisation-state'. As Pye put it, 'China is a civilisation pretending to be a nation'.[1] The PRC is the inheritor of a civilisation which has always seen itself as culturally superior, even if its 'humiliating' recent history has forced it temporarily to accept a lesser status. Signalling a change at the beginning of his term in office, President Xi Jinping announced that China was now on the road to revival and a 'great renewal of the Chinese nation'. The aim of foreign policy is to return China to the status to which it is entitled and to vanquish the remnants of its victimhood.

In his report to the 19th NPC in 2017, President Xi communicated his vision of China taking centre stage in the world. It would establish an alternative model to that of the West, in which collectivism trumps individualism, harmony reigns and coexistence replaces domination in international affairs. The Xi challenge resonates with a wider advocacy of Asian values that

Box 2.1   Ms Ao

Ms Ao is a sprightly eight-two-year-old retired university lecturer. She shares her sparsely furnished flat with her cat Mimi, paying a nominal rent to her former employers. Her living room is decorated with a large photograph of President Xi Jinping and a bright calendar depicting the *Liaoning*, China's first aircraft carrier, which was commissioned in 2012. A small Chinese flag is placed in the bowl of plastic fruit on her table. Ms Ao is deeply proud of her homeland and readily praises the virtues of the Communist Party. The former professor of philosophy has no time for what she calls revisionists trying to take from the victory of the revolution and is especially critical of Japan and the United States.

I am of the generation that fought to make new China. For more than one hundred years the Western countries humiliated us, attacked us and stole from us. Then Japan took advantage of us at our weakest point. They did terrible things to us, you have heard about Nanjing, but they did that everywhere. We fought them, defeated them and formed our New China. But still the Japanese want to attack us, they are so jealous of us they want to take our land. Our islands in the Pacific, which have always been part of China, they want to take, as they took our land before and it is the Americans who are behind it all. America is Japan's master and they are doing this for America. The Americans cannot bear to see China become great; they try to break us, to spread trouble in Xinjiang and Tibet, but they will never succeed in breaking the strength of the Chinese people.

Mahbubani and others claim are more appropriate for that region than the democratic values and institutions of the West: 'Europe should ... be ... a natural candidate to lead the world. For over two centuries, Europe has dominated world history ... Europe today is ... a model of rule-based society. It has woven an intricate set of regulations to govern behaviour among its members ... But Europe has not been able to extend its benign influence beyond its territory.'[2]

The ideological contest is reflected in China's domestic as well as foreign policies. In a new era of Socialism with Chinese Characteristics, the PRC would become more prosperous domestically and engaged internationally. Xi was clear that 'hard power' resources, such as military capacity, strong-arm diplomacy and economic sanctions, and more persuasive 'soft power' assets would both be employed. This chapter discusses how China uses these assets to promote its external goals.

Geopolitics

The current global footprint of China is relatively recent. Even now, the vast majority of Chinese live in the country's heartland, the North China Plain, dominated by the majority Han ethnic group and one of the most densely populated parts of the planet. To its north lies the Gobi Desert, to the west an increasingly hilly terrain that becomes the Tibetan plateau and to the south and south-east is the sea. Though this may seem a secure space in geopolitical terms, the Chinese themselves feel encircled and vulnerable.

No state has more neighbours than China and, since 1949, it has disputed the territorial border with most of them. The row with India continues to threaten military conflict.[3] On the whole, China's current stance in relations with Central Asia is dictated largely by issues of access to resources such as oil and gas, while other Asian countries are seen to present more pressing economic, political and security concerns.

China has long viewed itself as surrounded by nations friendly to the United States which allow US bases on their territory. China's more assertive South China Sea policy, for instance, is, to some extent, a response to the increased risk of a US-led encirclement, particularly after US President Obama's 'rebalancing to Asia' policy announced in 2014. The disputes about maritime delimitations and the sovereignty of offshore islands are, in part, about the rights of resource exploitation. More fundamentally, however, the strategy reflects a fear that, in a crisis, China may be deprived of energy security and maritime lines of communication. To forestall such a possibility, China is prepared to joust with its smaller South Asian neighbours, which have limited hard power resources. It may also challenge the current status quo with Japan, a country contemplating amending Article Nine of its 'pacifist constitution' renouncing war.

In the encirclement explanation, China's assertion of military control in the South China Sea is seen by President Xi as primarily a defensive tactic to protect its trade routes and territorial integrity. While, in contrast, joint naval exercises involving South Korea, the United States and Japan signal dangerous provocation. Similarly, though not presented in this way, the €7 trillion Belt and Road Initiative (BRI) (一带一路) may also be viewed as an attempt to counter the maritime advantage Western powers and their allies have enjoyed in recent centuries. The BRI encompasses projects not only in Asia but also in Africa, Europe and South America. Immediately, however, the restoration of land routes across Central Asia would return an element of China's historic strategic importance. In the near future, at least, Kazakhstan, the most prosperous and stable state in Central Asia, occupies a key strategic position for the BRI. China is, however, also investing heavily in the far-riskier enterprise of building transport infrastructure from Xinjiang to the Pakistani port of Gwadar on the Arabian Sea. This deep-sea facility would allow energy imports to reach China without having to transit through the Strait of Malacca, forming part of the 'string of pearls' hypothesis, which posits that China will try to expand its naval presence by building civilian maritime infrastructure along the Indian Ocean periphery.

In the designation 'hard power', economic sanctions are most effective when employed by the dominant partner in trade relations. In this respect, China uses its advantage to 'punish' countries that thwart its political priorities. This 'coercive diplomacy' is in contradiction to the official Chinese policy and is openly acknowledged. Indeed, China frequently frustrates the attempts of Western countries to impose economic sanctions on states that offend the global consensus. Nevertheless, China has, for example, shut off an oil pipeline to North Korea, threatened to suspend its exports of rare earth materials to Japan and imposed restrictions on banana imports from the Philippines. All these examples result from political disputes and reflect asymmetric interdependence in trading arrangements. While their bullying use is denied, such sanctions, or the implied threat of them, are an important aspect of Chinese hard power: 'The purposes of coercive diplomacy are either demand compliance from the targeted states or discouraging them from continuing certain policies.'[4]

The impact of this deployment is, therefore, hard to measure but as China's global trade increases, other states may be wary of triggering its ire by 'annoying' acts such as receiving the exiled Tibetan spiritual leader, the Dalai Lama, or giving too much credence to Taiwanese independence. At the same time, China itself may be slow to use its hard power in ways that contradict too easily its projected 'peaceful rise' image.

A critical test of China's ability to exercise its resources of either hard or soft power is North Korea, whose nuclear ambitions seem to threaten the security and stability in Northeast Asia. A nuclear arsenal based in a neighbouring state would challenge any Westphalian model, let alone China's proclaimed wish to respect national sovereignties. The possibility that Japan and South Korea would also acquire independent nuclear capabilities in response to the current threat could radically alter the current geopolitical balance. It may be a case where 'coercive diplomacy', though ostensibly denied, may be force-fully applied.

Much of the current government's policy stance seems a significant departure from Deng Xiaoping's 'lying low' inter-national strategy, aimed at securing a peaceful peripheral envir-onment to buttress economic development. The Deng approach underlined the practice of avoiding confrontation with America, Japan, India and other Asian nations and was punctuated with frequent declarations of peaceful intent and goodwill. In con-trast, President Xi has not shied from a higher level of insistence on China's territorial and maritime claims.

Military standing

In part to give credibility to the new bolder policy, President Xi has initiated a programme of modernisation of the PLA. Although the increase in annual military spending has recently slowed to around 7 per cent, only the United States expends more on its armed forces than China.[5] At an annual expend-iture of about €128 billion, the PLA has been able to acquire a whole assortment of the most modern weapons systems suited to a wide range of military use. Most notably, these assets have recently been used to shift the balance from China's traditional land-centric approach to one closer to that of America. The PLA is now being enabled to assert China's interests outside its boundaries. The forces have been reduced in personnel terms to about 2.25 million through re-organisation and efficiency measures, but it is still the world's most substantial military body. Importantly, however, the PLA is the armed force of the CCP, not, as in most countries, the State. The Party is clear that this status will not change, though it gives the military a direct voice in foreign policy. It also means that President Xi's reform of the PLA structure and his focus on corruption in the force reflect, in part, internal Party elements vying for influence. Indeed, the

2018 report of the CCDI, Xi's anti-corruption vanguard, specifically singled out 'interest groups' in the CCP as a core problem.[6] As mentioned earlier, some of the highest ranking and most powerful 'tigers' have been PLA generals.

The reforms were a source of tension in the ranks of the military, with some crucial changes of personnel, but the new structure puts the Central Military Commission (CMC) as the first tier, battle zone or theatre commands as second, with administrative supports in third place. The CMC is chaired by Xi Jinping, who also has the new title of commander-in-chief of the PLA. Leading military figures have been redeployed to reduce the possibility that pre-reform loyalties might hinder the changes and lessen the extent of CCP control. In a further indication of the thrust of the new military outlook, the resources balance between the various elements has recently favoured the navy ahead of the army and air force.[7]

'A military is prepared for war. All military works must adhere to the standards of being able to fight ... and win a war', Xi told the 19th NPC. 'Our army is the people's army; our defence is national defence. [We must] enhance ... national defence education, consolidate the unity between the military and civilian, in order to achieve the Chinese dream of a strong military.'[8] This Chinese Dream will be reflected in substantial military spending and organisational reform for some time to come. These changes mean that the 'PLA will able to be deployed to combat theatres more expeditiously than in the past'.[9]

The most immediate danger from Chinese military engagement is in the South China Sea, where a particular potential flash point is the oil drilling operations and Vietnamese bases in the Spratly Islands, an archipelago off the coasts of the Philippines, Malaysia and southern Vietnam. For China, Vietnam itself is no military threat, but any action risks involving the United States, Japan and other maritime powers. Trust between China and Vietnam has not recovered since anti-Chinese riots there in 2014 and all attempts at rapprochement have fundamentally failed.

Box 2.2   Anti-Japanese riots 2012

On 16 April 2012, Tokyo's right-wing governor Shintaro Ishihara announced that Tokyo Municipality would purchase a number of small privately owned islands in the Senkaku island chain (known as the Diaoyu Islands in China). The islands are part of the Ryukyu Islands archipelago, which has been ruled by Japan since the late nineteenth century but is claimed by China as part of its sovereign territory, stolen during the so-called 'century of humiliation'.

Tensions escalated to such an extent that by summer, violent riots broke out in cities across China. Protestors targeted visible Japanese symbols such as cars, while anti-Japanese protesters hurled ink bottles at the wall of the Japanese Consulate-General in Shenyang and also attacked the Japanese Embassy in Beijing. Troops were eventually called in to protect embassies and consulates while Japanese language schools were closed for a number of days at the height of the trouble.

The 2012 riots mirrored events which had taken place five years previously, sparked by protests over a Japanese school textbook which protestors claimed whitewashed Japanese atrocities during the Second World War.

One twenty-three-year-old female student in the central city of Xi'an, where some of the largest protests took place, described it as an anxious time:

> In our university, we were forbidden from attending the protests. Actually, the gates of the university were closed and we were not let out. I guess they were worried we would be hurt or maybe become involved in the violence. Many of my classmates were very angry, saying they hate the Japanese and would beat any Japanese.
>
> I don't have such strong feelings and violence is never okay but the Japanese have never apologised

> for what they did to us Chinese; until they do so,
> there will always be this tension. I am glad that my
> parents do not own a Japanese car!
>
> In late 2012, well-known entrepreneur Chen Guangbiao
> announced that he would personally replace the 173
> Japanese cars destroyed in the rioting, buying their owners
> Chinese-made Geely models instead.

Soft power

> We should increase China's soft power, give a good Chinese
> narrative, and better communicate China's messages to
> the world.
>
> (President Xi, 2014)[10]

According to Nye, 'success depends not only on whose army wins, but also on whose story wins' and China puts a great deal of effort into projecting its narrative abroad.[11] If power is about influencing people to act in your favour, then attraction and persuasion may be more important than military or even economic might.[12] China is among the countries that have taken this use of 'soft power' particularly seriously, pursuing it culturally, ideologically and developmentally. According to President Xi, a prominent national goal is to 'build our country into a socialist cultural superpower'.[13]

The core message resonates with the image of China as a 'civilisation-state' offering a counter to the pervasive influence of the West. For this reason, commentators in the West often underestimate China's soft-power imperative. The Chinese think of themselves as 'exceptional'. As Campbell points out: 'Since 1949, all Chinese schoolchildren have learnt in their history lessons that China ... "is a 3000-year-old civilization state".'[14]

In the Chinese case, there may be reason to accept the contention, given the country's antiquity and track record. From the soft-power perspective, the PRC is offering an alternative worldview to the liberal democratic model that has emerged in the West with its claim of universal values. The Party is the custodian and promoter of the message of culture and cohesion, not just within the confines of a nation-state but to the world. The target audience is both domestic and foreign and, according to President Xi, when addressing the 19th NPC: 'China's cultural soft power and the international influence of Chinese culture have increased significantly ... China's international standing has risen as never before.'[15]

Such assertions are difficult to measure but a crucial test for its soft power is how the citizens of other countries perceive China. In Africa, Latin America, Eastern Europe and parts of Asia, China is often viewed in a positive light, especially in contrast with the countries of Western Europe and North America. According to the survey evidence of the Pew Research Center:

> A median of 47% across the 38 countries surveyed has a favorable opinion of China, while 37% express an unfavorable view ... The most favorable views of China are found in sub-Saharan Africa ... where China has invested heavily in infrastructure and development. In Latin America, positive sentiment ... is highest in Peru ... In the Asia/Pacific region, opinion is mixed ... from a high of 64% in Australia to a low of 10% in Vietnam.[16]

The sustainability of positive responses from foreign publics in the wake of international events is problematic. Nevertheless, China's 'brand' is promoted vigorously by its government. As the CCP members at the 19th NPC were assured, by ministers quoting the Pew research, 'China has achieved greater soft power by developing its cultural industries and promoting international cooperation ... the country's cultural soft power has substantially increased since ... 2012, making vital contributions to the promotion of the causes of the Party and the nation'.[17]

In 2018, data from both the Edelman Trust Barometer and a Gallup poll showed that 'more people around the world considered China, rather than the US, a global leader'.[18]

The major weakness in China's soft-power arsenal is its perceived reliance on formal State agencies with little autonomy. Abroad, top-down initiatives may appear too much like avenues for propaganda rather than dialogue. Much of China's soft-power effort is directed by the United Front Work Department 中共中央统一战线工作部 of the CCP. The United Front's role has been enhanced by Xi Jinping but its increased functions have led to misgivings among its target audiences abroad. This is a particular problem for the Confucius Institutes, through which China seeks to extend its cultural reach. They partner with foreign universities and educational institutions to open Chinese language and cultural programmes. There are over 800 such arrangements worldwide. Unlike the Alliance Française, the British Council and the Goethe-Institut, however, that operate at 'arm's length' from their sponsoring government, each Confucius Institute is affiliated with the Ministry of Education of the PRC, from which it takes direction in policy and practice. Similarly, the proactive role of the State Council Information Office in keeping journalists, academics and others 'on message' means that much of the dialogue between Chinese agencies and citizens of other countries is suspect and its soft-power impact diminished.

To counter the effect of the West's global reach, China invests a great deal in the media. Ventures, such as the Xinhua News Agency, CCTV (China Central Television) and China Radio International, formerly known as Radio Beijing, try to match the performance values of foreign rivals in terms of ready availability, slick presentation and immediacy while staying as close as possible to an approved narrative. The congruence of official and media views may, however, be a disadvantage. As an experimental study on how news sources (Chinese versus American) were assessed showed, 'positive images or "soft power" for a foreign country [are] mediated by the audience's perceived trust in news coverage ... [P]ositive news about China did not always work in favor of the country's image'.[19] Trust in the source is an issue for the Chinese media because of the lack of anything approaching an independent relationship with the Party.

Among China's tactics as it engages in soft power offensives is the holding of mega-events, large-scale sporting, cultural and other gatherings that attract people directly or via the media as participants. Thus, the 2008 Beijing Olympics and the 2010 Shanghai Expo were two of the largest ever global events, and others have followed. In a study of Shanghai-related stories in thirty English-language newspapers in ten countries before, during and after Expo, Xue *et al.* found that it was a prominent item of news, that Shanghai's image was enhanced and the event had a significant impact on 'content and attitudes' of newspaper reports. They caution, however, that 'a single event cannot produce long-lasting effects'.[20]

A more long-term asset for Chinese soft power is the diaspora communities, estimated to be about sixty million in 180 countries, primarily in South-east Asia. Though 80 per cent of these overseas Chinese are not citizens of the PRC, policymakers stress the need to affirm the existing strong emotional ties. Xi Jinping remarked in 2014 that the overseas Chinese 'can play an irreplaceable role in realising the Chinese Dream of National Rejuvenation as they are patriotic and rich in capital, talent, resources, and business connections'.[21]

The United Front interacts with the diaspora by funding events, providing scholarships and facilitating business contacts. There have been suggestions, notably in Canada, New Zealand and Australia, that the overseas Chinese have been used for covert political purposes. According to Brady, 'New Zealand— along with other nations—is being targeted by a concerted foreign interference campaign by the PRC. The campaign aims to gain support for the CCP government's political and economic agendas by co-opting political and economic elites'.[22]

For the most part, however, the diaspora is employed as an avenue for cultural diplomacy and investment. While many ethnic Chinese abroad have no ambition to return to China and reject the label 'diaspora', the PRC sees them as an important niche market in its global diplomatic project.

For the civilisational State of China, the road to its revival is, in large part, taken to be a return to its rightful place in the world. The 'Middle Kingdom' will once more be a hub of scientific and cultural achievement and recognised as such by both its immediate neighbours and other potential rivals around the globe.

In achieving this renaissance and extinguishing the shame of the century of humiliation, the Communist Party will show itself to be worthy of support of the Chinese people. It will successfully have addressed the nationalist aspirations of citizens while, at the same time, securing their increased prosperity. In addition, by seeing its model adopted in the place of its Western counterpart, the CCP will enjoy the external validation that Chinese regimes have experienced over the centuries.

In Xi Jinping's China, nationalism plays a vital legitimising role. The narrative of great rejuvenation of the Chinese nation is that it can only happen under Communist Party rule and any threat to its hegemony is, by extension, a threat to China. Nationalism, of course, is an unstable element and, as the Japanese riots of 2005 and 2012 showed, can sometimes bubble up and descend into disorder and worse. The Chinese are rightly proud of their history, civilisation and the extraordinary growth of the past twenty years but, at times, this pride can lead to bellicose and even aggressive views. The danger for the CCP is keeping a lid on this and ensuring that the interests of the Party and nation are always seen as one and the same.

Notes

1   L. Pye, 'China: Erratic state, frustrated society', *Foreign Affairs*, 69:4 (1990), 56–74.

2   K. Mahbubani, *The New Asian Hemisphere: The Irresistible Shift of Global Power to the East* (New York, NY: Public Affairs, 2009), p. 237.

3   K. Richards, *China-India: An Analysis of the Himalayan Territorial Dispute* (Canberra: Centre for Defence and Strategic Studies, 2015).

4   C. Lai, 'Acting one way and talking another: China's coercive economic diplomacy in East Asia and beyond', *The Pacific Review*, 31:2 (2017), 1–19.

5   R. A. Bitzinger, *China's Defence Spending: Settling in for Slow Growth?* (Singapore: Nanyang Technological University, RSIS Commentaries, 42, 2017).

6   N. Gan, 'China's graft-busters set to finalise "super agency" plans as war on corruption hots up', *South China Morning Post* (9 January 2018), www.scmp.com/news/china/policies-politics/article/2127775/chinas-graft-busters-set-unveil-super-agency-war (last accessed 14 May 2018).

7   D. S. Rana, *The Current Chinese Defence Reforms and Impact on India* (New Delhi: Centre for Land Warfare Studies, 2017).

8   J. Dougherty, 'Chinese president makes upgrading military a priority', *Forward Observer* (21 October 2017), https://forwardobserver.com/2017/10/chinese-president-makes-upgrading-military-a-priority/ (last accessed 14 May 2018).

9   J. Char and R. A. Bitzinger, *New Direction in Strategic Thinking?* (Singapore: Nanyang Technological University, RSIS Commentaries, 218, 2017).

10 T. Barker, 'The real source of China's soft power', *The Diplomat* (18 November 2017), https://thediplomat.com/2017/11/the-real-source-of-chinas-soft-power/ (last accessed 14 May 2018).

11 J. S. Nye, 'Soft power: The origins and political progress of a concept', *Palgrave Communications*, 3 (2017), https://dx.doi.org/10.1057/palcomms.2017.8.

12 *Ibid.*

13 D. Shambaugh, 'China's soft-power push', *Foreign Affairs*, 95 (July/August 2015), 99–107, p. 99.

14 A. Campbell, *Defining China's 'Civilization State': Where Is It Heading* (Sydney: China Studies Centre, 2015), p. 2.

15 T. Mitchell and L. Hornby, 'Xi Jinping hails "new era" at opening of China congress', *Financial Times* (18 October 2017), www.ft.com/content/1fa302f6-b3b1–11e7-a398–73d59db9e399 (last accessed 14 May 2018).

16 R. Wike, J. Poushter, L. Silver and C. Bishop, 'Globally, more name U.S. than China as world's leading economic power', *Pew Research Center* (13 July 2017), www.pewglobal.org/2017/07/13/more-name-u-s-than-china-as-worlds-leading-economic-power/ (last accessed 14 May 2018).

17   Y. Hu, 'Nation boosts soft power', *China Daily* (22 October 2017), www.chinadailyhk.com/articles/4/44/209/1508643061066.html (last accessed 14 May 2018).

18   L. Zhou, 'Trust crisis in US institutions as Chinese confidence rises, Edelman global poll finds', *South China Morning Post* (22 January 2018), www.scmp.com/news/china/diplomacy-defence/article/2130081/trust-crisis-us-institutions-chinese-confidence-rises (last accessed 14 May 2018).

19   Y. Yuan, 'Soft power of international news media: American audiences' perceptions of China's country image mediated by trust in news' (Doctoral thesis, University of Maryland, 2017), https://drum.lib.umd.edu/handle/1903/19797 (last accessed 14 May 2018).

20   K. Xue, X. Chen and M. Yu, 'Can the World Expo change a city's image through foreign media reports?', *Public Relations Review*, 38:5 (2012), 746–54, p. 746.

21   R. Brown, 'What can India and China learn from each other about diaspora policy?', *The Diplomat* (2 February 2017).

22   A. M. Brady, 'Looking for points in common while facing up to differences: A new model for New Zealand-China relations', *Policy Brief no. 24* (University of Canterbury, New Zealand, 2017), p. 1.

3

People and place in the civilisation State

> I am very proud to be Chinese; China is more than my home, it is my mother and my father, it is as close to me as my own parents. Now we are strong again after over 100 years of humiliation, but we must never forget that weakness and never allow it to happen again. It is the dream of all Chinese people to see the country develop and become strong.
>
> (Wang, thirty-five-year-old businessman from Hunan province)

ON 8 August 2008, China wowed the world with a stunning opening ceremony for the Beijing Olympics. Directed by renowned film maker Zhang Yimou (张艺谋), the event involved some 15,000 performers and musicians showcasing a vibrant, confident nation proud of its history and culture. The ceremony, comprising two parts entitled 'Brilliant Civilization' and 'Glorious Era', was rich in nationalist imagery but noticeably short on Communist ideology. Confucius played a far greater role than Chairman Mao or Karl Marx. One section, in a display of national unity, saw fifty-six children from China's fifty-six national ethnic groups dressed in traditional costume carry the national flag into the stadium as nine-year-old Lin Miaoke performed 'Ode to the Motherland'. All was not quite as it seemed, however. In fact, these fifty-six children, while supposedly members of the ethnic groups they represented, were all from the Han majority. When this was put to Wang Wei, executive vice-president of the organising committee after the ceremony, he replied that it was 'traditional' to use dancers from other ethnic groups in this way: 'I would argue it is normal for dancers, performers, to be dressed in other races' clothes.'[1] In a further controversy, it turned out that Lin Miaoke was miming, having replaced the original singer Yang Peiyi – whose recorded song was still used – supposedly on the order of a senior official who did not believe Yang beautiful enough for the occasion.[2] The fact that the authorities would use children from the Han majority to represent those of minority ethnic groups such as Uyghur, Tibetan and Mongolian, can perhaps be interpreted as an example of the suspicion these groups are often held in by official China. It is hard to believe that the organisers were unable to arrange for children from each minority group to take part.

For most domestic viewers, the children represented a manifestation of national ethnic harmony where the fifty-five ethnic minorities, who in Chinese are known as the *Shaoshu minzu* (少数民族), joined their Han brothers and sisters in a display of the united *Zhonghua minzu* (中华民族), or national family. A complicated history of thousands of years during which dynasties expanded, retracted and collapsed numerous times while ruling over different regions has formed an ethnically complex and diverse nation. China's conceptualisation of itself as a multi-ethnic nation is based on Josef Stalin's 1953 definition of ethnic/national groups as those sharing a common territory, language and psychological nature.[3] This outlook is in line with Marxist history in which people progress from the primitive, feudal and capitalist up to the socialist modes of production. It marks where different populations had reached at the time of classification by Communist ethnographers.[4] This system led to the identification of fifty-six ethnic groups (which are rather confusingly often translated as 'nationalities'): fifty-five minorities and the Han majority, which today numbers 92 per cent of the population. Historically, China divided the world into a 'them' and 'us' dichotomy, of the civilised (文明) and the barbarian (野蛮人). The further you moved from the centre of China, the more uncivilised the people became.

Autonomy

In contrast to the Soviet Union, which established a system based on federal republics with a theoretical right to secession, the PRC instituted a system of limited territorial autonomy to manage ethnonational differences. Regional autonomy for ethnic minorities aims to give them economic, administrative and language privileges, but any discussion of self-determination is strictly prohibited. Today, China has five autonomous regions: the Tibetan Autonomous Region, Xinjiang Uyghur Autonomous Region, Ningxia Hui Autonomous Region, Guangxi Zhuang Autonomous Region and Mongolian Autonomous Region. In 2003, the Chinese government published a White Paper which states that 'since the Western Han Dynasty (206 BC–24 AD) [Xinjiang] has been an inseparable part of the multi-ethnic Chinese nation'.[5] It traces Chinese rule over the region to the present and declares it unbroken. This is the central aspect of government policy on all of the PRC's frontier regions. Xinjiang, Tibet and Inner Mongolia are now and have always been an inalienable part of the Motherland. There is and always has been 'one China'. To acknowledge otherwise would be to give credence to a view that China had, in fact, 'colonised' these vast areas.

From the beginning of the People's Republic, the issue of ethnicity was addressed in constitutional documents. *The Common Programme* promulgated in September 1949 promised all equal recognition, cultural autonomy and regional autonomy. Article 53 stated: 'All national minorities shall have the freedom to develop their dialects and languages, to preserve or reform their traditions, customs, and religious beliefs.'[6]

The rights of ethnic minority groups to use and be educated in their own language, to protect and preserve their culture and identify as an ethnic minority are also enshrined in the Chinese constitution. Similarly, the Law on Regional Ethnic Autonomy offers reassurance in areas including politics, economy, culture and societal issues. The People's Republic has also introduced 'positive action' – for example, policies which aim to increase minority access to education and economic opportunities. Some, such as the lower scores needed to enter university or less restrictive birth control policies, are controversial. Other policy initiatives aimed at increasing the number of ethnic minority cadres have met with limited success. Such peoples are rarely represented among the political or military elite in China. Since the founding of the PRC in 1949, only a handful of non-Han officials have been appointed to the Politburo and none to the elite level of the Politburo Standing Committee.

While relatively small proportionally, at just 8 per cent of the population, taken together the ethnic minorities of China would be the twelfth largest country in the world, coming between Mexico and the Philippines. The system of regional autonomy also means that China's five autonomous regions total 4.4 million sq. km out of the PRC overall, 9.6 million sq. km. Much of these areas are also rich in natural resources. As Mao put it: '[W]e say China is a country vast in territory, rich in resources and large in population; as a matter of fact, it is the Han whose population is large and the minority nationalities whose territory is vast and whose resources are rich.'[7]

Minorities in China are usually depicted as marginal and pre-modern. Gladney argues that the ethnic signifier of being Han has been fashioned with reference to the 'otherness' in the non-Han peoples of China.[8] This sense of the 'normal' and 'exotic' is directly related to the official portrayal of Han and minority groups in the PRC. By defining and representing minorities as exotic and primitive, it homogenised the majority as united, mono-ethnic and modern.

The Han

But what of the Han? How do the 92 per cent of Chinese fit into a system where all others are a small minority and they are overwhelmingly the largest and officially the most developed? There is a strong, and perhaps growing, sense of Han identity in China today. While the fifty-five ethnic minority groups are almost invariably depicted in colourful traditional costumes, usually in a pastoral setting, the Han, being the modern 'us' to the backward 'them', are typically shown in Western business suits or other fashionable attire. The 'advanced' in China means, invariably, 'Western-looking' and the Han represent modernity in the Western-style clothing which has long since replaced the military greens and greys of the Mao era for the vast majority of people.

However, one way in which a Han cultural renewal has come about is through the so-called 'hanfu revival' movement (汉服运动). This movement seeks to restore 'traditional Chinese culture' through the promotion of 'hanfu', claimed as the 'traditional ethnic clothing' of the Han Chinese.[9] While many choose to see it as nothing more than youthful dressing up, some have interpreted it as an example of Han nationalism that may harbour some deeper and more unsettling ideas with hints of the anti-foreigner sentiment of the nineteenth century. A twenty-five-year-old female university graduate in a large eastern Chinese city spoke of her participation in the movement and her reasons for joining:

> I am a member of this movement partly because I think the clothes look very beautiful and I really like the style but more importantly because it is my expression of who I am. It is very important that we understand and learn from our past and our culture. China has a very long history but most people in China do not have a good understanding of our culture. This is partly because during the Cultural Revolution, what was old was considered bad and dangerous and the people were made to forget. But even though people are free now to do as they please, they have turned their backs on much of their culture.
>
> When people wear what they think are traditional Chinese clothes, such as the qipao (旗袍), these are not genuine and authentic Han clothing. The qipao is something that foreigners designed in the early twentieth century; they are revealing and show the woman's body, they are certainly not traditional.

> There is so much emphasis on the minority culture and, of course, it is a good thing to help and to protect these minority cultures but the Han seem to have been forgotten. There is no attempt to protect our culture and if we do not try to do something about that we will lose who we are and become the same as the foreigners in everything we do.

This movement may owe much to a crisis of modernity or identification that is familiar to all young generations, combined with the Instagram generation's love of dressing up, yet scholars such as Carrico are concerned that movements such as this point to a broader and more confrontational nationalism that wishes to define China as a Han nation. He writes that the Chinese name for the movement, *Hanfu yundong*, highlights the two most important elements of this sociocultural phenomenon. On the one hand, as suggested by the term *Hanfu* (汉服; Han Clothing), the movement is dedicated to a rewriting of Chinese history around the central figure of the Han and a reinvention of Han traditions in the present. On the other hand, as indicated by the term *yundong* (运动; movement), this social group is a movement in the Maoist sense, insofar as it is dedicated to reshaping the world in its particular aesthetic image.[10] James Leibold has also argued that for many members of the movement, 'the category of the Han and its cultural attachments seem to provide a refuge – a sense of community, belonging and shared purpose – from the social dislocation, income disparity and market competition which marks the social malaise and tedium of modern urban life'.[11]

While a Confucian revival, sanctioned by Xi Jinping and the CCP, seems to be attempting to define itself as the natural successor to Confucianism, ethnic identity politics may not be something the authorities wish to encourage. Despite often being portrayed as a united and homogenous group, the reality is that the Han are made up of numerous sub-groups, such as the Hakka, Fujianese and Cantonese. They speak eight mutually unintelligible languages and show marked cultural diversity.

While an undoubted sense of pride in being Chinese is common to most, Chinese regional and linguistic differences run deep. A resident of Beijing speaking Mandarin will not understand a Guangdong lady's Cantonese, for example. Fingers drawing Chinese characters in the air or plotting out words on tables are a ubiquitous sight. While China has numerous dialects, all share the same written characters, *hanzi* (汉字).

Box 3.1   The China Nationalities Museum/ Chinese Ethnic Cultures Park, Beijing

Just down the street from Beijing's Olympic Stadium is the China Nationalities Museum/Chinese Ethnic Cultures Park. As the name itself suggests, it is simultaneously a 'museum' and a 'theme park', a fusion of the two. The park is owned and run by a for-profit State enterprise, the Chinese Nationalities Culture Park Corporation, and is spread over a large site of around 350 hectares. Each ethnic group is represented through 'typical' villages or individual dwellings dotted throughout the park amid water features, trees and flowerbeds. The correlation between ethnicity and 'landscape' is also evident in each area being called a 'scenic area'.

Here tourists can see members of each of the ethnic groups perform song and dance routines dressed in 'traditional costumes'. They can eat ethnic food and see inside the 'homes' of the ethnic people, even pose for photographs dressed in ethnic clothes. The park, in effect, brings the 'peripheries' into the 'centre', the remote and rural into downtown Beijing. While this is a tourist attraction, where paying visitors pose happily with young (usually female) minority peoples, it also has a clear educational mission which is stated in the visitors' brochure:

> The Cultural Park focus itself on an exhibition of ethnic architectures, preservation of minority cultural

heritage, propagation of anthropological knowledge, research of ethnic cultural heritage, enhance-
ment of ethnic cultures and promotion of unity of
nationalities. Combined landscapes with galleries
and interacted [sic] exhibition and dynamic
demonstrations, the Cultural Park records the past
and the present, by means of specific exhibitions on
environment, buildings, folk music and dances, food
cultures and traditional crafts, in order to provide
the visitors with opportunities for understanding of
diversified ethnic cultures and traditions.

While all fifty-six ethnic groups of the *Zhonghua minzu*
are supposedly represented, not all the ethnic scenic
areas are equally impressive. The Uyghur area is large
and consists of authentic-looking replicas of houses from
across the region and a mosque. Plaques indicate that
the structures were built by 'traditional craftspeople'. In
striking contrast to the 'authentic' Uyghur mosque, or the
'authentically constructed' replicas of the Uyghur houses,
is the Kazakh area. Represented by a single, cement 'yurt',
it is virtually indistinguishable from the Kirgiz yurt alongside it. Perhaps even more striking, the original Han scenic
area, marked on the map as one of the sites to visit, seems
to have been replaced by a Holiday Inn Hotel. Despite a
full day spent walking through the park, we never could
find if it had been moved elsewhere or disappeared into
the modernity of an American chain hotel.

Conflict

Despite the strong official narratives of ethnic harmony and unity,
China's two largest autonomous regions, Xinjiang and Tibet,
have a long history of ethnic conflict and violence. The riots
which erupted in Urumqi, the Xinjiang regional capital, on a hot
summer's evening in early July 2009, were the worst outbreak of

social unrest in China since the Tiananmen Square protests in 1989 and would have wide-ranging repercussions for local and national government. The official *China Daily* newspaper went so far as to describe the violence as the 'deadliest riot since New China was founded'.[12] According to official figures, the riots which broke out in some areas in the city of 2.3 million people left 197 people dead and over 1,700 injured. As the crisis deepened, then President Hu Jintao was forced to return to China from a G8 summit being held in Italy. While most of the fatalities occurred on the night of 5 July, it took three days and the deployment of thousands of People's Armed Police and regular soldiers onto the streets of Urumqi before the situation was brought under control.[13]

While 2009 was by the far the worst outbreak of violence in Xinjiang, there have been numerous other incidents. 2014 was a particularly violent year, when attacks spread from the region to Inner China, with an attack at Kunming train station killing over thirty and a suicide bombing at the symbolic heart of the Chinese nation, Tiananmen Square. The government has described the threat it faces in Xinjiang as coming from 'the three evil forces' of religious extremism, separatism and terrorism. Indeed, China has stressed vigorously that it is involved in its own 'War on Terror' in the region against an enemy similar to the one the United States and its allies have been fighting since the September 2001 attacks.

In August 2016, Chen Quanguo (陈全国), former Party chief of the Tibet Autonomous Region, replaced Zhang Chunxian (张春贤) as Xinjiang Uyghur Autonomous Region Party Secretary. Renowned as a hardliner, Chen had presided over a security crackdown credited by Beijing with ending a spate of self-immolations by monks in Tibet in 2012/13. Chen quickly introduced similar tactics to Xinjiang. According to James Leibold and Adrian Zenz, a total of 31,687 security-related job positions were advertised in 2016, a more than three-fold increase over the previous year.[14]

In April 2014, the *Xinjiang Daily* reported that more than 70,000 officials had been dispatched to villages and communities in Xinjiang in an effort 'to carry out a mass line campaign to boost development and people's livelihoods'.[15] These officials, many of them young university graduates unable to speak Uyghur, were sent to rural areas across Xinjiang. Usually stationed in police stations, they visit villages under armed police guard to promote government policies and monitor and correct 'undesirable behaviour and work styles'.[16] These tours of rural villages have led to tensions and in some cases violence.

February 2017 witnessed the largest military display of strength since the 2009 violence, when more than 10,000 troops gathered in the centre of Urumqi and some other cities across the region. Speaking at the rally, Party Secretary Chen vowed to 'bury the corpses of terrorists in the vast sea of the people's war [on terror]', while Deputy Party Secretary Zhu Hailun (朱海仑) declared that '[w]ith the caring and strong leadership of the Communist Party Central Committee, where President Xi Jinping serves as the core ... the strong support of 23 million people from all ethnic groups in Xinjiang, and with the powerful fist of the People's Democratic Dictatorship, all separatist activities and all terrorists shall be smashed to pieces'.[17] 2017 also saw the introduction of new anti-terrorist legislation which prohibits:[18]

- advocating or propagating extremist thoughts;
- wearing or forcing others to wear full-face coverings;
- hyping up religious fanaticism through growing beards or choosing names in an abnormal way;
- not allowing children to receive State education, interfering with State education;
- deliberately interfering or harming the implementation of family planning policies;
- publishing, downloading or reading articles, publications and audio-video material containing extremist content;
- rejecting or refusing State products and services that include radio and television programming.

In November 2016, it was also reported that the Shihezi Public Security Bureau Immigration Office had ordered Uyghur residents to surrender their passports for 'annual reviews'.[19]

Both Tibet and Xinjiang have seen a dramatic change in ethnic makeup, with large-scale Han migration to both regions leading to tensions and competition over resources. In 1949, the population of Xinjiang was 80 per cent Uyghur; it is just over 45 per cent today, with the Han now numbering almost 41 per cent. While Tibet has not attracted the same number of migrants, partly due to the difficulties of living at high altitude, the capital Lhasa is undergoing a dramatic rebuilding programme with department stores, towering residential blocks and hotels transforming it along the lines of any other Chinese city.

A twenty-eight-year-old Tibetan tour guide who studied at the spoke of his frustrations: 'We Tibetans are seen as a threat, the Uyghurs too, but we just want to live our lives in peace, to practice our religion and customs. But the government place so many restrictions on us, constantly monitor us, even the car I use to take tourists on trips has microphones so that they can check if I am saying something wrong.'

Despite the emphasis on ethnic harmony, distrust exists on all sides. A thirty-eight-year-old Han restaurant owner living in Xinjiang said: 'Unfortunately, many Uyghurs are thieves, it is their nature, and they have always been that way. Many Uyghurs make their living from stealing from people. I have been robbed in the past and so have many of my friends. It is not a case of education, they cannot be educated not to be thieves; they need to be severely punished and then they will learn.'

With the majority group occupying a position of 'most developed', indeed 'most civilised' in the Chinese sense, there is a risk that divisions between the groups could worsen. Prejudices and stereotypes are common, as are patronising attitudes. Some of these may result from China's somewhat contradictory approach to ethnicity, in which ethnic minorities are both separate and different, but also part of the national family. Some Chinese scholars, such as the sociologist Ma Rong, have called for a complete overhaul of the system and an end to official ethnic identifiers, favouring the more 'melting pot' approach of Europe.[20] There is unlikely to be a change in policy however, the authorities fearing that it would lead to more tensions rather than reducing them. More helpful might be a change in attitude.

One thirty-two-year-old Uyghur doctor explained: 'I am Chinese and I want to be proud of being Chinese. This is my home and we share so much here but the government make it seem like they only want me if I behave exactly like the Han, speak the language and give up on my customs and religion. They make it seem as if I cannot live here unless I live their way and that makes me very unhappy.'

Many countries survive deep cultural divisions by emphasising the everyday common interests and a shared investment in stability and prosperity. What marks China as different is the scale of its task – uniting a very dominant and self-confident ethnic group with a plethora of other identities that, while proportionately small, are numerically significant and often geographically concentrated. The task of uniting China has been taken up by the CCP. It offers a version of history and a take on global politics that stresses the advantages of One China and a social contract that encourages optimism and a commitment to prosperity and social mobility. It also punishes dissent and rewards loyalty. Like all monopolies, the Party is sensitive to potential rivals, accommodating to minor complaints but furiously protective of its dominant position. It is on its border regions of Xinjiang and Tibet that this social contract is perhaps at its weakest and where the government fears the potential for instability is greatest. These regions are far from the centre and occupied by peoples who historically did not consider themselves Chinese but to speak of these regions as being anything other than Chinese is to challenge to authorities in an unacceptable way.

The modern Chinese nation is one which has at its heart a seeming contradiction: on the one hand its people are one family united for thousands of years, but on the other its ethnic differences are stressed, even celebrated. All ethnic groups in China are equal but one is more developed than all others, and it is this older brother, the Han, who will help the minorities reach the stage of development the Han have achieved. To view it any other way is to threaten the unity of China and the harmony of its people.

Notes

1 S. Duclos, 'More Olympic fakery exposed: Ethnic children belonged to one group', *Digital Journal* (15 August 2008), www.digitaljournal.com/print/article/258624#ixzz4zSCxpD35 (last accessed 14 May 2018).

2 T. Branigan, 'Olympics: Child singer revealed as fake', *Guardian* (12 August 2008), www.theguardian.com/sport/2008/aug/12/olympics2008.china1 (last accessed 14 May 2018).

3 X. Zang, *Ethnicity in China: A Critical Introduction* (New York, NY: Wiley, 2015).

4 S. McCarthy, *Communist Multiculturalism: Ethnic Revival in Southwest China* (Seattle, WA: University of Washington Press, 2011).

5 The Information Office of the State Council, *The History and Development of Xinjiang* (Government White Paper, Beijing, 2003).

6 K. Palmer Kaup, *Creating the Zhuang: Ethnic Politics in China* (Boulder, CO: Lynne Rienner, 2000), p. 78.

7 Z. Mao, *The Writings of Mao Zedong 1949–1976: Vol II January 1956 – December 1957* (Armonk, NY: ME Sharpe, 1986), p. 43.

8 D. C. Gladney, 'Relational alterity: Constructing Dungan (Hui), Uygur, and Kazakh identities across China, Central Asia, and Turkey', *History and Anthropology*, 9:4 (1994), 445–77.

9 K. Carrico, *The Great Han: Race, Nationalism, and Tradition in China Today* (Oakland, CA: University of California Press, 2017).

10 *Ibid.*

11 J. Leibold, 'More than a category: Han supremacism on the Chinese Internet', *The China Quarterly*, 203 (2010), 539–59.

12 P. Foster, 'China riots: Worst outbreak of ethnic violence in 33 years', *Telegraph* (6 July 2009), www.telegraph.co.uk/news/worldnews/asia/china/5755863/China-riots-worst-outbreak-of-ethnic-violence-in-33-years.html (last accessed 14 May 2018).

13 D. O'Brien, 'The mountains are high and the Emperor is far away: An examination of ethnic violence in Xinjiang', *International Journal of Chinese Studies*, 2:2 (2011), 389–406.

14   A. Zenz and J. Leibold, 'Xinjiang's rapidly evolving security state', *China Brief*, 17:4 (2017), 21–7.

15   Quoted in X. Zhang, M. S. Brown and D. O'Brien, ' "No CCP, no New China": Discourses of pastoral powering the Xinjiang region of China', *China Quarterly* (Forthcoming, 2018).

16   *Ibid*.

17   T. Phillips, 'Chinese troops stage show of force in Xinjiang and vow to "relentlessly beat" separatists', *Guardian* (20 February 2017), www.theguardian.com/world/2017/feb/20/chinese-troops-stage-show-of-force-in-xinjiang-and-vow-to-relentlessly-beat-separatists (last accessed 14 May 2018).

18   Zhang *et al.*, ' "No CCP, no New China" '.

19   *Ibid*.

20   M. Rong, 'A new perspective in guiding ethnic relations in the 21st century: "De-politicization" of ethnicity in China', *Asian Ethnicity*, 8:3 (2007), 199–217.

4

Harmony and the self: rights and responsibilities

THE relationship between the State and the citizen in many modern societies is tutored by the notion that freedom and liberty are defined by privacy and personal autonomy. In the West, this is particularly true and is evidenced by the restrictions placed on agents of the government in their dealings with law-abiding citizens. In China, on the other hand, showing good behaviour is the sign of virtuous citizenship and reflects an optimistic Confucian view of human nature. Thus, aberrant behaviour is best addressed by society at large and watchfulness is a social duty. 'Compared with the West, Chinese society has developed a very different model of social control.'[1]

Similarly, the notion of 'rights', while often presented as universal and innate, is significantly different in Chinese culture, reflecting, as it does, contact with the West in the second half of the nineteenth century: 'the Chinese came to see rights as a way of augmenting power, enhancing the omnipotence of the state in its quest to unite and strengthen the Chinese nation, rather than a necessary restraint on state power as Locke envisaged'.[2]

China's citizens are some of the most heavily monitored people on earth with a reported twenty million surveillance cameras installed across the country in the last decade.[3] They are omnipresent, on every city street, in every residential compound, every school. In 2016, the Wuchang University of Technology, in the central province of Hubei, began using surveillance cameras to monitor its entire campus, including classrooms and dormitories. While some online commentators objected to students being treated like prisoners, others welcomed it as a means of ensuring good behaviour. A professor at the university, Sun Yi, was quoted on a local news website as saying it encouraged 'good study habits', while student Yan Yue said being placed under surveillance in the classroom had improved discipline and helped motivate students.[4] Other universities were quick to replicate, and it is now common throughout the country.

With the world's most restricted internet,[5] strict rules on household registration which leaves tens of millions of people technically living illegally in their own country, restrictions on the number of children couples can have and the numerous agencies tasked with monitoring and record keeping, the Chinese are perhaps the most policed people in the world. According to a study conducted at Tsinghua University, China spends over US\$77 billion on internal security or *weiwen* (维稳; stability maintenance) per year.[6] Since 2011, China has spent more on internal security than on its military, yet, despite the intrusive nature of much of the methods used, it is unusual to hear criticisms of an erosion of civil liberties. Privacy is still, to some degree, viewed with suspicion and the Chinese show a high degree of tolerance for what others would consider invasive and authoritarian.

In 2016, it was announced that China plans to develop a far-reaching social credit system which aims to build a culture of 'sincerity' and a 'harmonious socialist society', where 'keeping trust is glorious'. The hugely ambitious project aims to collect as much information as possible on each Chinese citizen and to award them a rating similar to a credit rating but based on 'social credit', which measures social as well as economic standing.[7] A whole range of privileges would be denied to those with a weak rating. The project aims to be in place by 2020.

China also leads the world in the development of facial recognition technology, which is being used in a range of diverse, sometimes comical, ways. The Temple of Heaven, one of Beijing's leading tourist attractions, has installed facial recognition to prevent overuse of toilet paper. People using the facilities will receive a sixty-centimetre serving of paper after they have conducted a facial scan; the software will deny the same person any more paper within nine minutes of their first scan.[8] China Construction Bank allows customers to pay with their faces at some vending machines, while Ant Financial, the online payments affiliate of e-commerce giant Alibaba, lets its 450 million users log in to their online wallets by taking a selfie.[9] You can even order and pay for a fried chicken meal at KFC by scanning your face at a restaurant terminal.[10] A joint project by the Ministry of Public security and a private security firm in Shanghai is aiming to build the world's most powerful facial recognition technology, capable of recognising any of China's 1.3 billion people within three seconds. According to the South China Morning Post, '[t]he system can be connected to surveillance camera networks and will use cloud facilities to connect with data storage and processing centres distributed across the country'.[11] The national system will contain the portrait information of every Chinese citizen along with detailed information on each. In December 2017, it was reported that authorities in the restive province of Xinjiang were collecting DNA and blood samples, as well as iris scans, from the entire population of twenty million.[12]

For many, this ever-present surveillance is a reassuring protection designed to keep them safe. The State is watching out for its citizens, as well as providing convenient ways to beat queues and increase efficiency. Mr Wang, a thirty-five-year-old taxi driver working in a medium-sized east coast city, but originally from a much more impoverished region, views the widespread monitoring as a positive way of ensuring people are kept safe:

> I think the cameras are very good. There are criminals and terrorists who want to attack us but the cameras help the police to keep us safe. There are some people in China who are lawless and uncivilised and they are dangerous. In a country with so many people, some of whom are still very poor, there are so many dangers. Take my taxi for example, by law I have to have cameras in it; this is to protect me in case I am attacked or robbed.

The imperative of security and monitoring is often consciously or unconsciously class-based. Every residential compound has a team of security guards, usually in police or military style uniforms, carefully monitoring who enters and leaves with particular attention given to those who look poor. Mr Zhu, a forty-five-year-old security guard, says: 'We have to be careful that those who are poor and dangerous do not come in. If you look at China, the crime is always carried out by poor people, they can be very resentful and this makes them dangerous. My job is to keep all of the residents safe and to protect their property. It is very important.'

China has a long history of strictly controlling the movement of its people. Despite some speculation in recent years that the system would be abolished, all Chinese citizens are still subject to the household registration system, or *hukou* (户口). Household registration has been in place in China for thousands of years but the current system was introduced in 1958 with the specific aim of preventing the rural poor from moving to the cities. The *hukou* identifies a person as a resident of a particular area of the country and includes basic information, such as date of birth and marital status. Residents may only access healthcare, education or other state-provided services in the place where they are registered. Despite this strict control, the number of migrant workers who have left the countryside in search of jobs now numbers over 160 million, accounting for 12.6 per cent of China's total population.[13] Most of these workers are technically living illegally and are unable to access services where they work. Their children are also unable to obtain education, meaning most leave their children in the care of grandparents in their home villages and return home to see them once a year at Spring Festival. It is estimated that more than sixty-one million children – about one-fifth of all children in China – live in villages without their parents.[14] It is perhaps unprecedented in human history that so many children have been raised apart from their parents; the repercussions both psychologically and socially will take some time to become apparent.

Internet

On the night of 5 July 2009, internet access was cut across the entire region of Xinjiang following riots in the provincial capital Urumqi. In the days that followed, these restrictions were extended to social networking sites such as Facebook, Twitter and YouTube throughout China. Along with numerous other news, social and file- and picture-sharing sites, they remain blocked in China. For almost one year, the internet was blocked entirely in Xinjiang, an unprecedented shutdown of the web which had an enormous economic impact and forced residents to undertake twenty-three-hour train journeys to the bordering province of Gansu just to access emails.[15] China may have the world's most substantial number of internet users, estimated at over 700 million,[16] but they access an internet which is more restricted than any other country apart from North Korea.

In a 2012 paper, Fan Dong of the University of Southern California outlined the various range of methods the authorities use to restrict internet content in China.[17] His research shows the 'Great Firewall of China', officially known as the 'Golden Shield' project 金盾工程 is far from a centrally organised whole, but instead something which varies from region to region in its effectiveness. The wall encompasses both high-tech scanning for trigger words, as well as an army of paid workers and volunteers who monitor and block content deemed sensitive or harmful. By blocking foreign social networking, like Twitter and Facebook, and forcing their citizens to use alternatives like Sina Weibo, China can control social networking sites, gaining the ability to censor posts, as well as access the vast amount of data these sites collect.

While the system has undoubtedly advanced since Dong's research, it remains strikingly arbitrary in its enforcement. Reports of suspected corruption from a top official may be accessed, while an Irish property rental company website cannot. The government and various local agencies may have invested millions, possibly billions, of dollars in attempting to control the internet but they are playing catch-up with technology which always seems one step ahead. Numerous virtual private networks (VPNs) can be accessed, some free, others for a small charge which allows users to overcome the restrictions. While these VPNs are widely used by foreigners living in China, Dong quotes a 2007 survey by the Chinese Academy of Social Sciences which found that only 0.6 per cent of Chinese internet users use VPNs frequently. A 2015 report that the government had vowed to clamp down on VPNs would suggest that the number has increased. The official English language *China Daily* reported that moves to block VPN services were for the 'healthy development' of the internet. In August of that year, all Xinjiang residents were required by the local government to download a mobile app that promised to 'clear the trash off your phone' but that, according to security experts, scans phones for digital fingerprints of illicit files, informing authorities when it finds them.[18]

As with other restrictions, there is evidence that Chinese citizens are in favour of strict control over the internet. Kou *et al.* suggest that even those who sometimes circumvent the system generally think it is a good thing: '[Their] complex, nuanced attitudes toward censorship resonate with the classic teachings of Confucianism, China's traditional philosophical and ethical system ... They viewed censorship as a government action to protect societal stability, even though they sometimes felt they needed to find ways around it.'[19]

A 2007 survey carried out by the Chinese Academy of Social Sciences found that 84.8 per cent of respondents believed that the government should be the primary body to regulate the internet.[20] The survey also found that 87 per cent of internet users would like to see pornography controlled, followed by violent content at 86 per cent, spam or junk mail at 83 per cent, advertisements at 66 per cent and slander against individuals at 64 per cent. Strikingly, just over 40 per cent believed that political content should be regulated, which was up from 12.4 per cent in a 2004 survey and 7.6 per cent in 2005, making it the fastest growing category across time. Research has also found that, although sceptical about the veracity of official reports, 'many Chinese citizens are even more reluctant to trust reports from international media organizations'. The 2007 report showed that

67.8 per cent of Chinese citizens trust national television news, while only 40.4 per cent trust international television sources; the trust in foreign newspaper and radio is even lower.

Surveys and reports carried out by official government-controlled agencies, such as the Chinese Academy of Social Sciences or the *People's Daily*, indicate that citizens are 'disciplined' and feel that the internet should be censored; however, these reports are unlikely to present a totally accurate picture. It is challenging to carry out reliable independent surveys on a topic considered extremely sensitive in China. Sun *et al.*'s 2012 study is an exception, attempting as it did to discover how free people living in urban China felt to express their opinions. The answer: not very. Only 21 per cent of respondents thought they could express their views about the government without reservations, with 12 per cent saying they are very cautious or never express their opinions about the government.[21]

The aforementioned Chinese Academy of Social Sciences report makes the point that, due to restrictions on content, the internet in China can be considered more an 'entertainment highway', rather than an 'information highway'. Thirty-two-year-old Miss Wang, who works for an international trade company in Shanghai, demonstrated this view:

> I use the internet for absolutely everything, it is how I do almost all of my shopping, how I communicate with my friends. When I have free time, I spend it online. Without the Internet, my life would be impossible, it would be so inconvenient. Our lives have changed so much in the past few years that it is now impossible to imagine how we lived before. My phone really is my life. But I don't care about politics or other things like that, they do not interest me and are not relevant to me so I don't care if I can't read about those things. I also think that there are many dangerous things on the internet that the government protect us from and that is very important.

However, there are also those who feel restricted by control, like many who have studied abroad. Miss Wang's twenty-seven-year-old colleague, Mr Xu, believes that the restrictions on the internet go too far.

> In China, we say that if you dam the river, it will eventually overflow and the control on information is like that. The government keep people in ignorance and hope that they will just use the Internet for leisure and to buy things but people care about more than that. Young people in China have been blinded by consumerism but there is so much that is unjust in this country, so much that cannot be hidden forever. In some countries, the internet is liberating but in China it binds us. But I don't think the government will always be able to control it.

A Maoist revival?

Xi Jinping has presided over a campaign that has seen the majority of dissenting voices silenced either through detention or fear. Numerous lawyers acting on behalf of those who have suffered in China's breakneck development have been arrested and imprisoned. During one weekend in January 2015, more than 200 civil rights defence lawyers were detained.[22] One of China's best known dissident voices, the Nobel Peace Prize winner Liu Xiaobo (刘晓波), died in prison in 2017, his supporters claiming he did not receive proper care and was not allowed to see his family. The internet, so vibrant commercially, is increasingly dark when it comes to any discussion outside of approved topics. More books are banned today than at any time since the Cultural Revolution (文化大革命, 1966–76). The government has also attempted to block foreign academic journals, such as the *China Quarterly*, which it says is undermining harmony by printing false research.

An official document that was leaked to the press and circulated widely, the so-called 'Document Number 9' warns against subversive currents in Chinese society. According to this document, there are seven currents in total, corresponding to the 'Seven Don't Speaks'. Among the forbidden topics are Western constitutional democracy, universal values of human rights, Western-inspired notions of media and civil society independence, ardently market-friendly neo-liberalism and 'nihilistic' critiques of the CCP's traumatic past. One of China's best-known journalists, Gao Yu (高瑜), was jailed for seven years in 2015 for leaking this document.

Third-level education, a particular area of concern for Xi Jinping, has also been targeted. In 2015, then education minister Yuan Guiren (袁贵仁) proposed what he called the 'two reinforcements' – namely, restricting the use of Western sources in teaching and the more aggressive pushing of official Communist ideology in universities: ' "Never let textbooks promoting western values appear in our classes," he said ... "Remarks that slander the leadership of the Communist Party of China" and "smear socialism" must never appear in college classrooms ... Teachers must "stand firm" and hold the "political, legal and moral bottom line".'[23] In 2016, the Education Ministry began requiring for the first time that universities make applicants who pass written exams submit to a personal interview meant to test their political fitness.

Despite such emphasis on stability maintenance and tight restrictions on media, internet and movement, violent events and protest are widespread. Some estimates suggest that there are over 500 'mass incidents' each day.[24] A 'mass incident' is officially defined as 'any kind of planned or impromptu gathering that forms because of internal contradictions', including mass public speeches, physical conflicts, airing of grievances or other forms of group behaviour that may disrupt social stability.[25] While many of these incidents are small-scale, some are large and violent, attracting international attention. Particular focus is paid to preventing any such events during critical political meetings and sensitive anniversaries like the 4 June anniversary of the Tiananmen Square massacre. Ahead of the NPC in October 2017, when Xi Jinping's leadership was further strengthened, enormous security was visible throughout the country and restrictions on the internet were particularly tight. At a meeting of the G20 group of world leaders held in the eastern city of Hangzhou in 2016, a third of the city's population of seven million was asked to leave for the duration of the event. The government gave them 2,000 yuan to spend on an enforced holiday, while 760,000 citizen volunteers were deployed to keep tabs on those that remained.[26]

China sees its citizens as requiring careful control and observation to prevent them from harming themselves and others. There is no place for civil liberties in this discourse. Even the idea of civil liberties is an alien and foreign idea which is included among the seven 'don't speaks'. The CCP portrays itself as a benevolent leader, kind and wise but intolerant of anything which may threaten the order of the nation. To question either the legitimacy of the CCP or the means it uses, is perceived as a threat to the State: 'Stability overrides all' (稳定压倒一切).[27] Increasingly, the Chinese government is attempting to eliminate even the possibility of such questioning, sometimes by force but also by persuasion: '[Officials] may be sent to the streets to buy off demonstrators, housing officials may be empowered to give rural evictees the right to move to cities, and retrievers may be paid bounties to surveil and inter-cept persistent petitioners to ensure that they do not make it to Beijing.'[28]

It is worth considering, however, that the very ideas of freedom and liberty, which have developed in the Western intel-lectual tradition from Enlightenment principles, are different in China. Edmund Fung writes of the Chinese idea of 'freedom as citizenship', that is that the central feature of freedom is a sense of social integration, solidarity and involvement con-ferred by membership in a nation. It entails a view of society in which the community is privileged over the individual.[29] For Fung, modern Chinese intellectuals conceived of freedom as a liberation movement rather than a conscious state of mind. While Europeans, building on the tradition of Locke, expounded theories of natural rights to justify the struggle for political freedom, Chinese thinkers located the essence of liberty in a specific context, namely resistance to tyranny – 'tyranny of rulers, familial control, feudalistic rituals, intellectual monism, and any repressive authority'.[30] In this understanding, freedom is the absence of the suffering and tyranny which had defined the nineteenth and early twentieth centuries. In official narratives, it is a freedom which can only be safeguarded by the Communist Party. One of the most common propaganda slogans in China is 'No CCP, No New China' (没有共产党就没有新中国).

Notes

1   X. Chen, 'Social and legal control in China: A comparative perspective', *International Journal of Offender Therapy and Comparative Criminology*, 48:5 (2004), 523–36, p. 526.

2   D. Cao, 'On the universality of "rights": Absence and presence of "rights" in the Chinese language', *Intercultural Pragmatics*, 14:2 (2017), 277–92, p. 228.

3   F. Langarett, 'In China, beware: A camera may be watching you', *National Public Radio* (29 January 2013), www.npr.org/2013/01/29/170469038/in-china-beware-a-camera-may-be-watching-you (last accessed 14 May 2018).

4   T. Phillips, 'Chinese university puts CCTV in dormitories to encourage "good study habits"', *Guardian* (16 June 2016), www.theguardian.com/world/2016/jun/16/chinese-university-students-cctv-surveillance-wuchang (last accessed 14 May 2018).

5   S. Croft, 'Internet censorship in China', *CNN* (6 July 2015), http://ireport.cnn.com/docs/DOC-1255127 (last accessed 14 May 2018).

6   Quoted in K. Kan, 'Whiter Weiwen: Stability mantainance in the 18th Party Congress era', *China Persepectives* (1 March 2013), http://chinaperspectives.revues.org/6120 (last accessed 14 May 2018).

7   S. Denyer, 'China's plan to organize its society relies on "big data" to rate everyone', *Washington Post* (22 October 2016),

www.washingtonpost.com/world/asia_pacific/chinas-plan-to-organize-its-whole-society-around-big-data-a-rating-for-everyone/2016/10/20/1cd0dd9c-9516-11e6-ae9d-0030ac1899cd_story.html?utm_term=.a6cb2618270c (last accessed 14 May 2018).

8   N. Connor, 'Beijing park uses face recognition software to wipe out toilet paper theft', *Telegraph* (20 March 2017), www.telegraph.co.uk/news/2017/03/20/beijing-park-uses-face-recognition-software-wipe-toilet-paper/ (last accessed 14 May 2018).

9   Y. Yang and Y. Yang, 'Smile to enter: China embraces facial-recognition technology', *Financial Times* (8 June 2017), www.ft.com/content/ae2ec0ac-4744-11e7-8519-9f94ee97d996 (last accessed 14 May 2018).

10 J. Mullen and S. Wang, 'Pay with your face at this KFC in China', *CNN* (1 September 2017), http://money.cnn.com/2017/09/01/technology/china-alipay-kfc-facial-recognition/index.html (last accessed 14 May 2018).

11 S. Chen, 'China to build giant facial recognition database to identify any citizen within seconds', *South China Morning Post* (13 October 2017), www.scmp.com/news/china/society/article/2115094/china-build-giant-facial-recognition-database-identify-any (last accessed 14 May 2018).

12 J. Griffiths, 'China collecting DNA, biometrics from millions in Xinjiang: Report', *CNN* (13 December 2017), http://edition.cnn.com/2017/12/12/asia/china-xinjiang-dna/index.html (last accessed 14 May 2018).

13 Statista, 'Migrant workers in China – statistics & facts' (31 May 2013), www.statista.com/topics/1540/migrant-workers-in-china/ (last accessed 14 May 2018).

14 W. Wan, 'In China, one in five children live in villages without their parents', *Washington Post* (30 December 2013), www.washingtonpost.com/world/asia_pacific/in-china-one-in-five-children-live-in-rural-villages-without-their-parents/2013/12/30/3f05a870-4b9a-11e3-9890-a1e0997fb0c0_story.html (last accessed 14 May 2018).

15 O'Brien, 'The mountains are high and the Emperor is far away'.

16 CIW Team, 'Total China internet users reached 751 million in H1 2017', *China Internet Watch* (4 September 2017),

www.chinainternetwatch.com/22235/751mn-h1–2017/ (last accessed 14 May 2018).

17 F. Dong, 'Controlling the Internet in China: The real story', *The International Journal of Research into New Media Technologies*, 18:18 (2012), 403–25.

18 E. Feng, 'Security clampdown bites in China's Xinjiang region', *Financial Times* (14 November 2017), www.ft.com/content/ee28e156–992e-11e7-a652-cde3f882dd7b (last accessed 14 May 2018).

19 Y. Kou, B. Semaan and B. Nardi, 'A Confucian look at Internet censorship in China' (Conference paper, given at the 16th IFIP TC.13 International Conference on Human-Computer Interaction, Mumbai, India, 25–29 September 2017).

20 Dong, 'Controlling the Internet in China'.

21 W. Sun, X. Wang and Y. Zhou, 'How free do people feel to express their opinions? A study in urban China', *Applied Economics Letters*, 19:12 (2012), 1165–9.

22 L. Hornby, 'Chinese media publishes lawyer's confession', *Financial Times* (19 July 2015), www.ft.com/content/d74ae90a-2e1b-11e5–91ac-a5e17d9b4cff (last accessed 14 May 2018).

23 Agence France-Presse, 'China says no room for "western values" in university education', *Guardian* (30 January 2015), www.theguardian.com/world/2015/jan/30/china-says-no-room-for-western-values-in-university-education (last accessed 14 May 2018).

24 K. J. O'Brien and Y. Deng, 'Preventing protest one person at a time: Psychological coercion and relational repression in China', *The China Review*, 17:2 (2017), 179–201.

25 T. Ran, 'China's land grab is undermining grassroots democracy', *Guardian* (16 December 2011), www.theguardian.com/commentisfree/2011/dec/16/china-land-grab-undermining-democracy (last accessed 14 May 2018).

26 T. Phillips, 'Ghost town: How China emptied Hangzhou to guarantee "perfect" G20', *Guardian* (5 September 2016), www.theguardian.com/world/2016/sep/05/ghost-town-how-china-emptied-hangzhou-to-guarantee-perfect-g20 (last accessed 14 May 2018).

27 T. Cliff, *Oil and Water: Being Han in Xinjiang* (Chicago, IL: University of Chicago Press, 2016), p. 192.

28 O'Brien and Deng, 'Preventing protest one person at a time', p. 180.

29 E. Fung, 'The idea of freedom in modern China revisited: Plural conceptions and dual responsibilities', *Modern China*, 32:4 (2006), 453–82, p. 456.

5

To get rich is glorious

'To get rich is glorious' (致富光荣), often attributed to Deng Xiaoping (邓小平), marked a critical change in Chinese politics that proclaimed that socialism was not incompatible with a market economy. It signalled a new pragmatic approach to policy that diverged dramatically with the Maoist dogmatic ideological line. Its impact transformed the politics of everyday life in China. Questions remain, however, about the PRC's capacity to sustain its economic momentum and how this new wealth is divided.

In the decades after 1980, the annual growth rate in China approached an average of 8.7 per cent. In modern times, no other country of any size has experienced anything like it. While in recent years, the performance has slowed, China's record is phenomenal. The economy was expanding at around 7 per cent in 2017, comfortably above the government's target. Not since the Han dynasty (206 BC to AD 220) has China been so prosperous and, like their imperial predecessors, the current regime appreciates the link between economic success and political stability. Nevertheless, economic performance is not the only relevant criterion. Regime legitimacy in China has historical and philosophical roots that outweigh short-term prosperity. Particularly in the Confucian tradition, the bond with the people hinges on the morality of the political elite, benevolent governance, as well as material well-being.[1] Crucially, the

Box 5.1   Ms Wang

In 2003, Ms Wang lived in a small garage on the ground floor of an apartment building in the suburbs of an eastern coastal city. The premises were intended for bicycle storage, but Ms Wang had set up a small general provisions store there supplying the surrounding apartments with instant noodles, beer, chilli flakes and other essentials. She also lived there, sleeping on a little foldout camp bed at the back. Suffocating in the summer and freezing in the winter, it was, however, a liberating business for the woman who had recently moved from the north-eastern province of Liaoning following a messy divorce. Her thirteen-year-old son, who spent most of the year studying at a martial arts school in another city, came back during holidays and wowed neighbours with his nunchuck skills and high kicks outside of his mother's store. Ms Wang was a warm, kind-hearted lady who quickly made friends and who worked extremely hard in her tiny illegal shop.

On a return visit to the neighbourhood ten years later, we attempted to find Ms Wang and sought out her store. As we wandered, trying to remember where it was, we were suddenly met with a warm cry. She had seen and recognised us. She was indeed still living in the neighbourhood, but she proudly told us, no longer in the garage. Now she owned five apartments, drove a Range Rover and ran a highly profitable import–export company specialising in all things Japanese. She wore a diamond necklace and insisted on bringing us for dinner to a ludicrously expensive restaurant where we were joined by her son, now a grown man and manager of her company. Ms Wang's was an extraordinary story since she left the poverty of her home village in the north-east, a journey shared by countless others but also a journey which has left many behind.

public's judgement of the central government is often at odds with that applied more locally. Beijing may be assumed to be ignorant of the misdeeds of local officials who 'appear to have absorbed the brunt of Chinese citizens' political frustration ... most Chinese citizens ... trust central leaders more than the local authorities'.[2]

'All politics is local'

Though there is no doubting the power of the central government, much of the institutional force behind China's success is decentralised and often located at the provincial level. Even at the city tier, mayors compete to facilitate investment, to encourage local economic growth and safeguard local fiscal revenues. Importantly, given the performance measures for state officials, deal-making with business interests can enhance their career prospects. Some of the initiatives taken at the local level amount to corruption and provoke the ire of citizens but much of it is productive. In an authoritarian system, however, 'the ability to encourage innovation (and capture good ideas) is vital to continued success' both economically and politically.[3] The Xi Jinping campaign for greater probity may have the unintended consequence of inhibiting risk-taking and experimentation among local officials. To date, however, the self-interest of local officials in meeting their targets has dramatically incentivised economic development. Indeed, in a rare public rebuke, China's central bank chief suggested that their enthusiasm for new projects and the loans to support them were the 'root cause of the country's financial fragility'.[4]

Although geography is important, a motivated and capable local leadership, open to new ideas, can make a significant difference to how any particular locality thrives.[5] Economy-boosting development zones and infrastructural investment often reflect the efforts of enterprising local officials to champion their areas. As in many political and economic systems, however, there is a tendency for development to be greatest in the regional core city, usually the provincial capital. So that, even at an intra-provincial level, peripheral locations are inclined to be less prosperous. 'China has shifted from one of the most egalitarian countries in terms of distribution of life satisfaction to one of the least egalitarian ... In particular ... life satisfaction has declined markedly in the lowest-income segments of the population, while rising somewhat in the upper socioeconomic status stratum.'[6]

China remains a profoundly unequal society with striking and disturbing contrasts of wealth and poverty on display in every city. The richest 1 per cent of households own a third of the country's wealth, while the poorest 25 per cent have just 1 per cent, a 2016 study from Peking University found.[7] China's Gini co-efficient for income, a widely used measure of inequality, was 0.49 in 2012, according to the report. The World Bank considers a co-efficient above 0.40 to represent severe income inequality. Among the twenty-five largest countries by population, for which the World Bank tracks Gini data, only South Africa and Brazil are higher at 0.63 and 0.53, respectively. The figure for the United States is 0.41, while Germany is 0.3. Such widespread inequality has, of course, led to social tensions which can at times spill out into open conflict. Two people on very different sides of China's social divide expressed some of these strains. A twenty-five-year-old university student from a prosperous east coast city said: 'The trouble is there are many bad people among these people [the poor]; they lack quality and do not know how to behave. They can be loud and dirty, and sometimes they are involved in crime. I think it would be a good idea for middle-class people to live in one area and the lower classes live in another separately. That way the police can monitor them more easily and keep the society more harmonious and civilised.'

Yes, that is a young, wealthy university student calling for the establishment of ghettos so that he and his class can be kept away from the poor. He is, as it also happens, a proud member of the Party.

A forty-five-year-old female cleaner in the same city had a very different perspective:

I am proud to be a worker. Chairman Mao told us to learn from the peasants and workers. My family have always been farmers [in Anhui province], but now that there is more money to be made in the city we have moved here. Our lives are much more comfortable now, we have some money and can buy some small things. I enjoy my job, but sometimes people do not respect me, they talk down to me or ignore me. This makes me sad. My generation would always appreciate older people, but some of these students think we are servants. Our China has changed so much.

Social contract

An important part of the social contract between the CCP and the people is the expectation of continually improving material welfare. In the past, the instruments of social welfare, guaranteed employment and minimum income, may have fulfilled this commitment. Today, however, the affluence enjoyed by many Chinese and the heightened expectations of others reflect an economy based on profit, risk and the other imperatives of a free economic structure. Politically, the system is characterised by the hope of social mobility and the maintenance of trust. The Party-State seeks to maintain the loyalty of critical sections of society by anticipating and attending to their needs. High on the list of beneficiaries of this approach is the expanding middle class, but the process of governance is very complicated and not all policy decisions can be explained by the need to placate the powerful or potentially troublesome.

To garner support, the Party points to the way it has guided China from the tragedy and poverty that were associated with social experiments, like the Great Leap Forward; (1958–62), to the affluence of the east coast cities and their hinterlands. For most of the citizens, the social contract's condition of material improvement has been met in considerable part. Since its transition from a centrally planned economy to a free market one, and particularly following the reforms initiated by Deng, the Chinese economy has grown exponentially. Some of this growth is attributable to strategic investment in state-owned enterprises (SOEs), the liberalisation of commercial laws and regulations, as well as exceptional increases in labour productivity. Additionally, a significant facet has been the opening up of the Chinese economy to foreign direct investment. From the 1990s on, international companies have become significant drivers of the Chinese economy.

There are reasons to be concerned about the future trajectory of the economy, as wages in China are now considerably higher than in some competitor countries, such as India. Further, though it is relatively young at the moment, the workforce has been declining since 2012. In addition, as a result of the strict one-child policy, the dependency ratio may become burdensome in the foreseeable future – the so-called '4–2–1 problem', where one child must look after two parents and four grandparents. Of course, labour costs could be lowered if companies relocated inland to avail of cheaper prevailing rates, but such adjustments would provide only temporary respite. The dominant business strategy has been to move upmarket and become less reliant on low wage costs. This is disruptive in the short term, but the alternative could be to go out of business. Politically, especially for state-owned firms, an immediate reaction to commercial pressure may be seen in discretionary subsidies or other barriers to trade. SOEs may also avail of cheaper land and capital access, often from state-owned banks that are responsive to government priorities. There is evidence of all these options in some sectors but, as a sustainable policy response, they are expensive and short-term. In his report to the 19th NPC in 2017, Xi Jinping made clear that his priorities included economic reforms and rebalancing. Given that his grip on power was emphatically confirmed by the Congress, Xi may feel more confident in adopting a longer-term view on economic policy.

Ideologically, the changes are described as a move towards a 'socialist market economy', one in which the government 'has the capacity to shape economic outcomes', as well as the intention to do so.[8] For the average Chinese citizen, however, the experience is of consumer choice and ready availability on a par with that in major capitalist economies. Similarly, while SOEs are strategically important, most businesses are privately owned and in tune with market imperatives. The scale and rapidity of the changes are reflected in the fact that food rationing was only finally ended in 1993. Indeed, the reform of the agricultural sector in the early 1980s saw both food production and labour availability for manufacturing increase.

A characteristic of the Chinese experience, however, remains proactive state involvement. Even though significant adjustments may be indicated by orthodox economic theory, the politics of everyday China means that discontinuities in growth and expansion must be avoided. Socio-economic uncertainty is perceived as a threat to regime stability, so confidence in positive growth must be encouraged, even as it slows to some degree. The strength of this imperative was felt in the period after the 2008 collapse of many Western economies. The CCP was not in a position to guide China through a time of economic realignments with widespread redundancies and significant social welfare adjustments. It, therefore, responded to the downturn by increased government spending and investment. As a result, though export markets were in turmoil, the average Chinese worker did not experience the kinds of painful changes associated with this period elsewhere in the world. Scholars suggest that, while the radical reform of the late 1970s and the early 1980s may have been affirmed politically, incremental economic change is the currently favoured prescription. This is particularly true for the urban middle class, which, like its counterparts elsewhere, is burdened by mortgages and other ongoing financial commitments.

Box 5.2   Wang Li and Gu Bing

Wang Li and his new bride Gu Bing are both twenty-three-year-old Shanghai natives, newly married and very much in love. They are also extremely worried about debt. The couple, who met while studying at university, have recently bought their first apartment together in a modest Shanghai neighbourhood, near to a metro line, but between one and two hours from their respective jobs. While they are both highly educated, neither is making much more than the Shanghai average monthly wage of RMB 9,000 (€1,142). Their tiny one-bed 50 sq. m apartment cost significantly more, however, than the average price per square metre of RMB 94,000 (€11,930). The couple, like most, borrowed much of the money from their parents and other family members but also, as is increasingly common, took out a large bank loan to make up the difference.

'If we want to live in Shanghai near our families, then we have to spend so much money on this apartment. It is quite frightening', Wang Li says. 'We could never have afforded a place on our salary, not if we saved for twenty years. There is nothing luxurious about our place; it is simple and small. Everybody in China feels this pressure now, but it is so bad in Shanghai. At least the pressure is less to pay back our parents, but the bank is very worrying. We are stressed all the time. We aim to be able to buy another apartment eventually and rent this one out, that way we can have children and maybe our parents can live with us when they are older.'

'There is so much pressure in everyone's life now', Gu Bing says. 'You have to be able to show that you are successful, that you have a good apartment, that you are investing, that you are driving a nice car. Otherwise, you are seen as a failure. There is so much pressure on young people to be seen as a success, but the wages don't match with these pressures, so everybody is borrowing all of the time. The cars, the apartments, even clothes, people are borrowing all this money. They think it is easy and cheap, but it really is not. Maybe because we Chinese don't have experience of borrowing we are less careful, but I am very worried about this. My husband and I think about debt all the time.'

In China, the 'subordinate' class, as Goodman describes them, constitutes around 85 per cent of the population.[9] Many may aspire to upward social mobility, hard work and greater consumption but, for the Party, it is important to monitor the disposition of those who may harbour resentment or a sense of injustice and, even more alarmingly, display a propensity for protest. Such disquiet may reflect the perceptions that CCP members and their families are enriching themselves at the expense of the people generally; income inequalities are growing but are ignored by the State; and, that disparity is sharpening. The Party ideology that emphasises the historical role of the working class jars with many who observe the 'triumphant bourgeoisie'. Indeed, between 1978 and 2015, factors such as high saving and investment rates and changes in relative asset prices have helped the share of the PRC's wealth, owned by the top 10 per cent of earners, move from 27 per cent to 41 per cent. At the same time, the bottom 50 per cent stake fell from 27 per cent to 15 per cent. As Piketty *et al.* put it: 'China's inequality levels used to be close to Nordic countries and are now approaching U.S. levels.'[10] Addressing this trend was a central theme in President Xi Jinping's report to the 19th NPC in 2017. Couching his remarks in a Marxist idiom, he said: 'What we now face is the contradiction between unbalanced and inadequate development and the people's ever-growing needs for a better life.'[11]

One group that feels particularly deprived of its historic mission in ideological terms is the rural population. Tellingly, the rural community is outside the CCP's favoured urban support base and politically marginalised. The *hukou*, or household registration system, links peoples' access to services to their residential status as urban or rural. Notwithstanding the rural roots of the CCP, farmers were, for decades, ignored by the social security framework set up to reassure urban workers, but were not regarded as a danger by the Party-State. Even when rural protests occurred, they were seen as isolated and locally containable. In the Chinese historical narrative, farmer uprisings have been associated with collapsed dynasties and regime change but, for the modern state, the rural disturbances were seen as primarily aimed at local government and easily dealt with using the targeted arrests of leaders, preventing crowds gathering and intensified monitoring. Nevertheless, advocates of a more liberal understanding of the challenges facing the rural poor have had an impact that does not reflect a simple political cost–benefit analysis. Recently, targeted social policies have been introduced that provide a more generous level of health and pension support. Similarly, experimental schemes aimed at improving basic educational provision and removing vexing and sometimes arbitrary rural taxation have been extended across the PRC. These policy changes illustrate the role that astute advocates can have, even in a highly centralised system with a keen sense of vulnerability.[12]

An issue that links the rural population to the cities and does evoke a clear political response is food safety. Taking on the trad-itional Chinese role as benevolent leader of the huge empire, the CCP is under enormous pressure. The integrity of the food supply has always been high on the implied contract between governments and their citizens but, in China, the issue also has deep cultural and historical significance. From the Song Dynasty (960–1279), when China experienced a doubling in population, until today, Chinese governments have been judged in large part by their management of the food supply. Food scandals under-mine the ethical foundations of the modern Chinese society at a time when the Chinese leadership is re-inventing itself as the pro-vider of a harmonious and just society. The Party is an assiduous user of market research, and it knows that issues of food safety rank with corruption as a significant public concern, especially among the urban population.[13] The CCP response is illustrative of the thrust of policy in politically sensitive areas. Strict new laws, draconian penalties and high-profile punishment of officials, in the Legalist tradition, are trumpeted. Self-regulation and voluntary measures that could facilitate state-wide networks are eschewed.[14]

In the food area, tiny farms and local enterprises dominate the production process and distribution channels with scant cap-acity for record keeping and little traceability. Ominously for the CCP, many of the food contamination incidents have triggered domestic public protest and unrest. Food is also a proxy for discontent for a rural population that resents the growing gap between their lot and the ever more prosperous urban dwellers. Farmers see the new food safety regulations as onerous and mostly unnecessary – imposed by corrupt local officials for the benefit of urban Chinese.

The food safety example points to the influence of international agencies on Chinese domestic policy. 'Made in China' used to signal a need for caution to foreign consumers as it became associated with cheap and often shoddy products. Today, its connotations are much less unfavourable as the PRC has progressively become integrated into global agencies for quality assurance and dispute arbitration, such as the WTO and GATT. Indeed, 'Made in China 2025' (中国制造 2025) is the title of an important ten-year national plan that outlines China's objectives in the development of manufacturing. It is modelled on Germany's 'Industry 4.0' plan and was issued by the State Council in 2015.

As a major exporter, Chinese labour conditions are now open to scrutiny and potential loss of brand image. As a result, domestic policies around labour conditions reflect foreign anxieties as well as local pressures. Embarrassment at low rankings in international standards measures can also expedite policy change. Cases of poor quality in food imports and foreign restaurant chains are also publicised in China as a way of 'measuring' the progress made under the strict new laws and regulations.

The need for the Party-State to be seen to protect its citizens from the cyclical economic patterns that have been so costly for administrations in Europe and elsewhere has encouraged a proactive approach to potential downturns. It has, however, significantly increased the amount of government debt at all levels. The magnitude of debt in the PRC is of global significance, but Chinese officials charged with its management suggest that, in the context of growth, the danger of a 2008-type crisis is low. China has ample debt capacity. Nevertheless, for SOEs and local government, the burden is real and masks substantial overcapacity in some areas and gross inefficiencies in others.

The air we breathe

In March 2015, an internet documentary by one of China's leading journalists, Chai Jing, that outlined in graphic detail the devastation China's air pollution is causing to its people, was viewed over 100 million times in forty-eight hours.[15] The documentary was eventually blocked by the authorities, nervous that a major backlash was building.

There can be no doubt that China's environment has suffered horrific damage since the reform and opening-up period. After years of denial, the government has now acknowledged the vast scale of the problem. Air pollution alone kills hundreds of thousands per year, with almost none of China's cities considered safe in terms of air quality by WHO standards. Estimates, including health costs and loss of productivity due to pollution, range between 3 and 6 per cent of China's total GDP each year.[16]

In March 2014, Premier Li Keqiang (李克强) declared a 'war on air pollution', promising that the government would come down with an 'iron fist' against polluters. The plan was for the country to cut coal consumption by 220 million metric tonnes.[17] Since then, there has been genuine success and it is notable in major cities that the air has improved, especially in the most polluted winter months. However, it remains a heavily polluted country by any measure. China's cities regularly top lists of the world's most polluted and air purifiers, face masks and mobile phone apps telling the day's pollutant levels are a part of life. It is also becoming apparent that while the major cities of the east coast are improving, the pollution is spreading to once clean western regions. In a 2016 Greenpeace report, the five cities with the highest levels of PM2.5 particulates – small enough to deeply penetrate the lungs – were all in the westernmost region of Xinjiang. Kashgar in Xinjiang's south-west was by far the most polluted city, with an average PM2.5 concentration of 276.1 microgrammes per cubic metre for the three months of that year, up 99 per cent on the same period in 2015.[18]

A thirty-two-year-old ethnic Uyghur businessman from Urumqi spoke of his anger at this:

They are moving all the dirty polluted industry from the eastern cities to Xinjiang and Tibet. When the leaders wake up in Beijing they can smell the poison in the air, they worry about their children and grandchildren, more than that they worry about the rich people getting angry, so they send their filth to here, where we are poor and voiceless. That is the way, that is what they think of us and it makes me so angry. The rich Han will save themselves by killing us.

Exporting overcapacity

Business decisions in China generally reflect market conditions, forecast demand, etc., in much the same way as in most ostensibly capitalist countries. There is, however, a further consideration, especially when the enterprise is state-owned. Political priorities, as defined by the CCP, are also taken into account. As a result, some businesses are too valuable even to falter while others are viewed as long-term bets to be sheltered from direct market forces. Thus, for example, overcapacity in solar energy companies may seem a temporary problem in the context of global warming. A consequence of excess current output in this and other sectors is the need to find outlets for production. China's international trading partners often suggest that it is, in effect, selling below the cost of production to alleviate domestic pressure at the expense of foreign rivals. For instance, the government's thirteenth Five-Year Plan (2016–2020), a significant policy document in today's China, called for the steel industry to be regulated in ways that are in line with sustainable development. China is the world's largest producer of the metal, and a slowdown could have positive effects on a global market suffering from oversupply.[19] Affected industrialists and their provincial governments have, however, managed to circumvent the plan in the name of regional prosperity and to trade directly with foreign markets.[20] In such cases, where powerful Party interests circumvent the economic logic, China's domestic politics is paramount even at the expense of strong objections by foreign governments. As President Xi stressed in 2016, SOEs are 'the major force to boost the comprehensive strength of the country and to protect the common interests of the people'.[21] They are strategically important, large-scale and capital-intensive and thus too valuable to be left to the vagaries of market forces alone.

The increasingly prominent role of the Party in SOEs is, in part, attributable to the impetus of President Xi's anti-corruption drive discussed earlier. It is, however, also a sign that the government in Beijing wishes to tighten its control as part of a wider political process of industrial transformation. The 100 largest SOEs have changed their articles of association to reflect the new modus operandi of Party vetting decisions ahead of formal management approval. The Party is purporting to be taking a more comprehensive and long-term perspective on economic matters that is tutored by ecological and responsiveness to popular opinion. The current Five-Year Plan, for example, includes targets for pollution abatement. It is, of course, also keen to forestall the disruption that may be the product of market forces alone. Such a proactive stance is, in effect, a characteristic of a 'socialist market economy' as understood in today's People's Republic. Nevertheless, speaking of SOEs at the 19th NPC, President Xi promised to develop 'mixed-ownership economic entities, and turn Chinese enterprises into world-class, globally competitive firms'.[22]

Real estate

A significant contributory cause of the 2008 financial crisis in the West was a sharp rise in mortgage lending to households. The household debt to asset ratio was unsustainable in many countries. Many observers point to similar patterns in both urban and rural China: 'In many respects, China looks like a classic housing bubble. Housing prices have soared. New construction is enormous. Vacancies are large and pervasive. It is tempting to ... conclude that a price drop is imminent.'[23]

Between 2003 and 2014, house prices rose annually by more than 10 per cent in real terms. While demand is still strong, some purchases are clearly speculative. Government action may be needed to prevent a crisis that will be all the more important because of its significance for the Party's valued middle-class support. The housing market's Chinese characteristics include a wide range of tenure types and a division of responsibilities between local and central government. Nevertheless, President Xi's regime is keenly aware of the importance of the issue and is trying to stabilise the market with initiatives ranging from loosening controls on the rental sector to building new satellite cities around Beijing. At the end of 2017, the IMF warned that China's credit to GDP ratio is now about 25 per cent above the long-term trend. This is very high by international standards and consistent with a high probability of financial distress and that the pressure to maintain the country's rapid growth has bred an unwillingness to let struggling firms fail.[24]

'To get rich is glorious' and to prosper is fine too but, for some commentators, the process was thought to be a dangerous one for the one-party state. If, as consumers, life was full of choice and economic opportunity, would Chinese citizens not eventually baulk at their lack of political options and question the Party monopoly? If the life of the people was, in fact, only about material advancement, this might indeed be a threat to the CCP. In everyday politics, however, much more is on offer. The China of Xi Jinping also allows citizens to benefit from pride in their nation and safeguards against foreign encroachment by following the ideological certainties of Socialism with Chinese Characteristics. Their country has thrown off humiliation and, they are assured, is heading inexorably back to its rightful place at the centre of global politics.

Yet pressures and challenges abound: the desperate pollution of China's cities, its devastated natural environment and the soaring rates of inequality risk provoking instability. A thirty-three-year-old father of two surnamed Hu from southern Jiangxi province explained:

I have always supported the Party. I am a Party member as my father is and my grandfather. My grandfather was a member of the PLA, a hero who fought the Japanese and the Kuomintang. But in 2008 there was a scandal, baby milk formula was poisoned and the government covered it up, my own son drank that milk, he was sick, he was lucky to survive. Since then I have doubted much. The government can do so much but they are not able to stop the poison that we breathe; my children cough all the time. Shopping centres and luxury apartments are no good if we are too sick to enjoy them. This is my greatest fear, that my children will become sick. Your views change when you have children.

Notes

1   Y. Tong, 'Morality, benevolence, and responsibility: Regime legitimacy in China from past to the present', *Journal of Chinese Political Science*, 16:2 (2011), 141–59.

2   E. Cui, R. Tao, T. J. Warner and D. L. Yang, 'How do land takings affect political trust in rural China?', *Political Studies*, 63:51 (2015), 91–109.

3   J. Teets, 'The politics of policy innovation in China: Local officials as policy entrepreneurs', *Issues & Studies*, 51:2 (2016), 79–109, p. 79.

4   J. Cai, 'The root cause of China's financial fragility – according to its central bank chief', *South China Morning Post* (7 November 2017), www.scmp.com/news/china/economy/article/2118656/root-cause-chinas-financial-fragility-according-its-central-bank (last accessed 14 May 2018).

5   X. Shen and K. S. Tsai, 'Institutional adaptability in China: Local developmental models under changing economic conditions', *World Development*, 87 (2016), 107–27.

6   S. Zhou and X. Yu, 'Regional heterogeneity of life satisfaction in urban China: Evidence from hierarchical ordered logit analysis', *Social Indicators Research*, 132:1 (2017), 25–45, p. 25.

7   G. Wildau and T. Mitchell, 'China income inequality among world's worst', *Financial Times* (14 January 2016), www.ft.com/content/3c521faa-baa6-11e5-a7cc-280dfe875e28 (last accessed 14 May 2018).

8   B. Naughton, 'Is China socialist?', *The Journal of Economic Perspectives*, 31:1 (2017), 3–24.

9   D. S. G. Goodman, *Class in Contemporary China* (London: John Wiley, 2014).

10   T. Piketty, L. Yang and G. Zucman, 'Capital accumulation, private property and rising inequality in China, 1978–2015', *NBER Working Paper No. 23368* (Cambridge, MA: National Bureau of Economic Research, 2017), p. 2.

11   Xinhua, 'Principal contradiction facing Chinese society has evolved in new era: Xi', *China Daily* (18 October 2017), www.chinadaily.com.cn/china/19thcpcnationalcongress/2017–10/18/content_33401026.htm (last accessed 14 May 2018).

12   J. Duckett and G. Wang, 'Why do authoritarian regimes provide public goods? Policy communities, external shocks and ideas in China's rural social policy making', *Europe-Asia Studies*, 69:1 (2017), 92–109.

13   X. Wu, D. L. Yang and L. Chen, 'The politics of quality-of-life issues: Food safety and political trust in China', *Journal of Contemporary China*, 26:106 (2017), 601–15.

14   N. Collins and J.-C. Gottwald, 'Being well fed: Food safety regimes in China', in T. Havinga, F. van Waarden and D. Casey (eds), *The Changing Landscape of Food Governance* (Cheltenham: Edward Elgar, 2015), pp. 78–95.

15   C. Hutton, 'Under the Dome: The smog film taking China by storm', *BBC China Blog* (2 March 2015), www.bbc.com/news/blogs-china-blog-31689232 (last accessed 14 May 2018).

16   B. Schwartlander, 'Are we losing the war on pollution?', *China Daily* (6 January 2017), www.chinadaily.com.cn/china/2017–01/06/content_27881815.htm (last accessed 14 May 2018).

17   Q. Wang, 'China to "declare war" on pollution, cut energy use', *China Daily* (14 March 2014), www.chinadaily.com.cn/china/2014npcandcppcc/2014–03/14/content_17346330.htm (last accessed 14 May 2018).

18 Agence France-Presse, 'China air pollution shifts west in first quarter: Greenpeace', *Yahoo* (20 April 2016), www.yahoo.com/news/china-air-pollution-shifts-west-first-quarter-greenpeace-061449483.html (last accessed 14 May 2018).

19 M. Pooler, 'Chinese steel production to slow sharply in 2018', *Financial Times* (9 January 2018), www.ft.com/content/7dfb918e-f087–11e7-b220–857e26d1aca4 (last accessed 14 May 2018).

20 H. Choi and S. Lee, *Using Modified Anti-Dumping Mechanisms for Sustainable Development: The Case of the Chinese Iron and Steel Industry* (Seoul: The Asian Institute for Policy Studies, 2017).

21 T. Mitchell, 'China's Communist party seeks company control before reform', *Financial Times* (15 August 2017), www.ft.com/content/31407684–8101–11e7-a4ce-15b2513cb3ff (last accessed 14 May 2018).

22 Xinhua, 'Xi calls for furthering SOE reform', *China Daily* (18 October 2017), www.chinadaily.com.cn/china/2017–10/18/content_33403609.htm (last accessed 14 May 2018).

23 E. Glaeser, W. Huang, Y. Ma and A. Shleifer, 'A real estate boom with Chinese characteristics', *Journal of Economic Perspectives*, 31:1 (2017), 93–116, p. 114.

24 L. Elliot, 'China's debt levels pose stability risk, says IMF', *Guardian* (7 December 2017), www.theguardian.com/world/2017/dec/07/china-debt-levels-stability-risk-imf (last accessed 14 May 2018).

Conclusion

POLITICS of China continues to be the subject of a vast academic literature. Much of this analysis is constructed around statistical and other research that tracks the PRC's economic, diplomatic and cultural achievements. It is also often couched in comparative terms that seek to plot China's changing geopolitical role. This book aims to add to that body of knowledge by focusing on the experience of Chinese people in their everyday lives. It has sought to trace the politics of China as it is experienced on a day-to-day basis by both its citizens and those who control the institutions of government.

Ordinary individuals seek to conduct their lives in the context of the political system – complying and complaining as circumstances allow. They make the best of their positions in the light of their station in life. Like their counterparts elsewhere, they avail of the advantages the State offers and try to minimise any disadvantages to themselves. Sometimes, they bypass the authorities altogether using the informal social networks in the way Chinese people have always done. The calculations they make are not necessarily conscious ones, but they reflect the range of broader values evident in Chinese society. Some of these norms have their roots in dynastic times far removed from the modern age.

Even in a relatively authoritarian political system, such as that of the PRC, those responsible for government also try to make the system work with the highest level of voluntary compliance and widespread support that they can achieve. They too share a pride in a Chinese civilisation often rooted in past achievements and relish its 'return' to its rightful place in the world order. They are wary of anything that remotely poses an existential threat to Party rule but, once reassured, seek to respond to public concerns.

It is 'normal' for politics to seem complicated and confusing. The immediate exposure to politics comes through the traditional and social media, as well as the interaction with state employees. Much of the most influential political science literature on countries throughout the world focuses on how citizens seek to make sense of passing events on the basis of little knowledge and rudimentary understanding. Like ordinary people elsewhere, the Chinese are busy with the pressing issues of their everyday lives and use various cognitive devices to fit politics into their broad understanding of the world. Critical to the Chinese is a sense of their country's role in history. China has, in their view, always been at the cutting edge of science, technology and economic development. Its culture has similarly led the way in terms of achievement and sophistication. The century of humiliation is recognised as an anomaly currently being rectified by the Chinese collectively, and individually under the leadership of the Party-State. Emotions, such as pride, nationalism and fear of change, are closely tied to the politics of everyday life and the CCP understands the role of sentiment.

Chinese people are not complacent about the issues of corruption, inequality and ethnic tension but see them as being addressed both practically and philosophically in the context of an ancient norm of civilisation. As in previous periods, food safety, personal debt and job insecurity are pressing issues for almost everyone. History has visited her problems on China before, but it also offers a resource for understanding the politics of everyday life. Thoughts of Confucius and the achievements of ancient dynasties remain an asset on which to draw. Despite predictions of its demise due to the contradictions between a market economy and an autocratic regime, the Party is, for the most part, able to rely on ready compliance with public policy. Having said that, the CCP is conscious of how the apparently stable states of Communist Eastern Europe, and the USSR itself, imploded with such speed.

In the accounts given here, there is little suggestion that China's political system is about to make way for a liberal democratic market-based alternative. The regime, though ever more intrusive, commands widespread support in the majority population. Nevertheless, a prosperous China is likely to be one in which everyday politics is typified by more material choices, more national pride, but also greater expectations of the State. The public agenda may be amended to make environmental concerns, corruption and nationalism more prominent but the Party's record of responsiveness to everyday concerns suggests political continuity rather than change.

Further reading

Breslin, S. *China and the Global Political Economy* (London: Palgrave Macmillan, 2013).

Brown, K. *The New Emperors: Power and Party in China* (London: I.B. Tauris, 2014).

Collins, N. and A. Cottey. *Understanding Chinese Politics* (Manchester: Manchester University Press, 2012)

Gamer, R. (ed.). *Understanding Contemporary China* (Boulder, CO: Lynne Rienner, 2014).

Guo, S. *Chinese Politics and Government: Power, Ideology and Organization* (London: Routledge, 2013).

Joseph, W. A. *Politics in China: An Introduction* (Oxford: Oxford University Press, 2014).

Lieberthal, K. *Governing China: From Revolution Through Reform* (New York, NY: W. W. Norton, 2004).

Mitter, R. *Modern China: A Very Short Introduction* (Oxford: Oxford University Press, 2016).

Saich, T. *Governance and Politics of China* (London: Palgrave, 2015).

Spence, J. *The Search for Modern China* (London: W. W. Norton, 2013).

Zang, X. *Understanding Chinese Society* (London: Routledge, 2011).

Bibliography

Agence France-Presse. 'China says no room for "western values" in university education', *Guardian* (30 January 2015), www.theguardian.com/world/2015/jan/30/china-says-no-room-for-western-values-in-university-education (last accessed 14 May 2018).

Agence France-Presse. 'China air pollution shifts west in first quarter: Greenpeace', *Yahoo* (20 April 2016), www.yahoo.com/news/china-air-pollution-shifts-west-first-quarter-greenpeace-061449483.html (last accessed 14 May 2018).

Barker, T. 'The real source of China's soft power', *The Diplomat* (18 November 2017), https://thediplomat.com/2017/11/the-real-source-of-chinas-soft-power/ (last accessed 14 May 2018).

Bitzinger, R. A. *China's Defence Spending: Settling in for Slow Growth?* (Singapore: Nanyang Technological University, RSIS Commentaries, 42, 2017).

Brady, A. M. 'Looking for points in common while facing up to differences: A new model for New Zealand-China relations', *Policy Brief no. 24* (University of Canterbury, New Zealand, 2017).

Branigan, T. 'Olympics: Child singer revealed as fake', *Guardian* (12 August 2008), www.theguardian.com/sport/2008/aug/12/olympics2008.china1 (last accessed 14 May 2018).

Branigan, T. 'Xi Jinping vows to fight "tigers" and "flies" in anti-corruption drive', *Guardian* (22 January 2013), www.theguardian.com/world/2013/jan/22/xi-jinping-tigers-flies-corruption (last accessed 14 May 2018).

Brown, K. 'The Communist Party of China and ideology', *China: An International Journal*, 10:2 (2012), 52–68.

Brown, R. 'What can India and China learn from each other about diaspora policy?', *The Diplomat* (2 February 2017).

Cai, J. 'The root cause of China's financial fragility – according to its central bank chief', *South China Morning Post* (7 November 2017), www.scmp.com/news/china/economy/article/2118656/root-cause-chinas-financial-fragility-according-its-central-bank (last accessed 14 May 2018).

Campbell, A. *Defining China's 'Civilization State': Where Is It Heading* (Sydney: China Studies Centre, 2015).

Cao, D. 'On the universality of "rights": Absence and presence of "rights" in the Chinese language', *Intercultural Pragmatics*, 14:2 (2017), 277–92.

Carrico, K. *The Great Han: Race, Nationalism, and Tradition in China Today* (Oakland, CA: University of California Press, 2017).

Char, J. and R. A. Bitzinger. *New Direction in Strategic Thinking?* (Singapore: Nanyang Technological University, RSIS Commentaries, 218, 2017).

Chen, S. 'China to build giant facial recognition database to identify any citizen within seconds', *South China Morning Post* (13 October 2017), www.scmp.com/news/china/society/article/2115094/china-build-giant-facial-recognition-database-identify-any (last accessed 14 May 2018).

Chen, X. 'Social and legal control in China: A comparative perspective', *International Journal of Offender Therapy and Comparative Criminology*, 48:5 (2004), 523–36.

China Daily. 'Full text of Hu Jintao's report at 17th Party Congress' (7 September 2010), www.chinadaily.com.cn/china/19thcpcnationalcongress/2010–09/07/conten_29578561_8.htm (last accessed 14 May 2018).

Choi, H. and S. Lee . *Using Modified Anti-Dumping Mechanisms for Sustainable Development: The Case of the Chinese Iron and Steel Industry* (Seoul: The Asian Institute for Policy Studies, 2017).

CIW Team. 'Total China internet users reached 751 million in H1 2017', *China Internet Watch* (4 September 2017), www.chinainternetwatch.com/22235/751mn-h1–2017/ (last accessed 14 May 2018).

Cliff, T. *Oil and Water: Being Han in Xinjiang* (Chicago, IL: University of Chicago Press, 2016).

Collins, N. and J.-C. Gottwald. 'Being well fed: Food safety regimes in China', in T. Havinga, F. van Waarden and D. Casey (eds), *The Changing Landscape of Food Governance* (Cheltenham: Edward Elgar, 2015), pp. 78–95.

Connor, N. 'Beijing park uses face recognition software to wipe out toilet paper theft', *Telegraph* (20 March 2017), www.telegraph. co.uk/news/2017/03/20/beijing-park-uses-face-recognition-software-wipe-toilet-paper/ (last accessed 14 May 2018).

Croft, S. 'Internet censorship in China', *CNN* (6 July 2015), http:// ireport.cnn.com/docs/DOC-1255127 (last accessed 14 May 2018).

Cui, E., R. Tao, T. J. Warner and D. L. Yang. 'How do land takings affect political trust in rural China?', *Political Studies*, 63:51 (2015), 91–109.

Denyer, S. 'China's plan to organize its society relies on "big data" to rate everyone', *Washington Post* (22 October 2016), www.washingtonpost.com/world/asia_pacific/chinas-plan-to-organize-its-whole-society-around-big-data-a-rating-for-everyone/2016/10/20/1cd0dd9c-9516–11e6-ae9d-0030ac1899 cd_story.html?utm_term=.a6cb2618270c (last accessed 14 May 2018).

Denyer, S. 'China's president takes campaign for ideological purity into universities, schools', *Washington Post* (12 December 2016) www.washingtonpost.com/world/chinas-president-takes-campaign-for-ideological-purity-into-universities-schools/ 2016/12/12/2395ec42-c047–11e6-b20d-3075b273feeb_story. html (last accessed 14 May 2018).

Dong, F. 'Controlling the Internet in China: The real story', *The International Journal of Research into New Media Technologies*, 18:18 (2012), 403–25.

Dougherty, J. 'Chinese president makes upgrading military a priority', *Forward Observer* (21 October 2017), https://forwardobserver. com/2017/10/chinese-president-makes-upgrading-military-a-priority/ (last accessed 14 May 2018).

Duckett, J. and G. Wang. 'Why do authoritarian regimes provide public goods? Policy communities, external shocks and ideas in China's rural social policy making', *Europe-Asia Studies*, 69:1 (2017), 92–109.

Duclos, S. 'More Olympic fakery exposed: Ethnic children belonged to one group', *Digital Journal* (15 August 2008), www.digitaljournal.com/print/article/258624#ixzz4zSCxpD35 (last accessed 14 May 2018).

Elliot, L. 'China's debt levels pose stability risk, says IMF', *Guardian* (7 December 2017), www.theguardian.com/world/2017/dec/07/china-debt-levels-stability-risk-imf (last accessed 14 May 2018).

Feng, E. 'Security clampdown bites in China's Xinjiang region', *Financial Times* (14 November 2017), www.ft.com/content/ee28e156–992e-11e7-a652-cde3f882dd7b (last accessed 14 May 2018).

Foster, P. 'China riots: Worst outbreak of ethnic violence in 33 years', *Telegraph* (6 July 2009), www.telegraph.co.uk/news/worldnews/asia/china/5755863/China-riots-worst-outbreak-of-ethnic-violence-in-33-years.html (last accessed 14 May 2018).

Freeden, M. *Ideology: A Very Short Introduction* (Oxford: Oxford University Press, 2003).

Fung, E. 'The idea of freedom in modern China revisited: Plural conceptions and dual responsibilities', *Modern China*, 32:4 (2006), 453–82.

Gan, N. 'China's graft-busters set to finalise "super agency" plans as war on corruption hots up', *South China Morning Post* (9 January 2018), www.scmp.com/news/china/policies-politics/article/2127775/chinas-graft-busters-set-unveil-super-agency-war (last accessed 14 May 2018).

Gladney, D. C. 'Relational alterity: Constructing Dungan (Hui), Uygur, and Kazakh identities across China, Central Asia, and Turkey', *History and Anthropology*, 9:4 (1994), 445–77.

Glaeser, E., W. Huang, Y. Ma and A. Shleifer. 'A real estate boom with Chinese characteristics', *Journal of Economic Perspectives*, 31:1 (2017), 93–116.

Goodman, D. S. G. *Class in Contemporary China* (London: John Wiley, 2014).

Griffiths, J. 'China collecting DNA, biometrics from millions in Xinjiang: Report', *CNN* (13 December 2017), http://edition.cnn.com/2017/12/12/asia/china-xinjiang-dna/index.html (last accessed 14 May 2018).

Hirschman, A. O. *Exit, Voice, and Loyalty: Responses to Decline in Firms, Organizations, and States* (Boston, MA: Harvard University Press, 1970).

Holbig, H. 'Ideology after the end of ideology: China and the quest for autocratic legitimation', *Democratization*, 20:1 (2013), 61–81.

Hornby, L. 'Chinese media publishes lawyer's confession', *Financial Times* (19 July 2015), www.ft.com/content/d74ae90a-2e1b-11e5–91ac-a5e17d9b4cff (last accessed 14 May 2018).

Horwitz, J. 'Beijing is evicting its migrants and displacing its e-commerce couriers', *Quartz* (27 November 2017), https://qz.com/1138278/beijing-is-evicting-its-migrants-and-displacing-its-e-commerce-couriers-who-work-for-companies-like-alibaba-and-jd/ (last accessed 14 May 2018).

Hu, Y. 'Nation boosts soft power', *China Daily* (22 October 2017), www.chinadailyhk.com/articles/4/44/209/1508643061066.html (last accessed 14 May 2018).

Huang, Z., 'What you need to know about Beijing's crackdown on its "low-end population"', *Quartz* (22 November 2017), https://qz.com/1138395/low-end-population-what-you-need-to-know-about-chinas-crackdown-on-migrant-workers/ (last accessed 14 May 2018).

Hutton, C. 'Under the Dome: The smog film taking China by storm', *BBC China Blog* (2 March 2015), www.bbc.com/news/blogs-china-blog-31689232 (last accessed 14 May 2018).

The Information Office of the State Council, *The History and Development of Xinjiang* (Government White Paper, Beijing, 2003).

Jin, K. 'The Chinese Communist Party's Confucian revival', *The Diplomat* (30 September 2014), https://thediplomat.com/2014/09/the-chinese-communist-pa (last accessed 14 May 2018).

Kan, K. 'Whiter Weiwen: Stability mantainance in the 18th Party Congress Era', *China Persepectives* (1 March, 2013), http://chinaperspectives.revues.org/6120 (last accessed 14 May 2018).

Kou, Y., B. Semaan and B. Nardi. 'A Confucian look at Internet censorship in China' (Conference paper, given at the 16th IFIP TC.13 International Conference on Human-Computer Interaction, Mumbai, India, 25–29 September 2017).

Lai, C. 'Acting one way and talking another: China's coercive economic diplomacy in East Asia and beyond', *The Pacific Review*, 31:2 (2017), 1–19.

Langarett, F. 'In China, beware: A camera may be watching you', *National Public Radio* (29 January 2013), www.npr.org/2013/01/29/170469038/in-china-beware-a-camera-may-be-watching-you (last accessed 14 May 2018).

Leibold, J. 'More than a category: Han supremacism on the Chinese Internet', *The China Quarterly*, 203 (2010), 539–59.

Mahbubani, K. *The New Asian Hemisphere: The Irresistible Shift of Global Power to the East* (New York, NY: Public Affairs, 2009).

Mao, Z., *The Writings of Mao Zedong 1949–1976: Vol II January 1956 – December 1957* (Armonk, NY: ME Sharpe, 1986).

McCarthy, S. *Communist Multiculturalism: Ethnic Revival in Southwest China* (Seattle, WA: University of Washington Press, 2011).

Mitchell, T. 'China's Communist party seeks company control before reform', *Financial Times* (15 August 2017), www.ft.com/content/31407684–8101–11e7-a4ce-15b2513cb3ff (last accessed 14 May 2018).

Mitchell, T. and L. Hornby. 'Xi Jinping hails "new era" at opening of China congress', *Financial Times* (18 October 2017), www.ft.com/content/1fa302f6-b3b1–11e7-a398–73d59db9e399 (last accessed 14 May 2018).

Mullen, J. and S. Wang. 'Pay with your face at this KFC in China', *CNN* (1 September 2017), http://money.cnn.com/2017/09/01/technology/china-alipay-kfc-facial-recognition/index.html (last accessed 14 May 2018).

Naughton, B. 'Is China socialist?', *The Journal of Economic Perspectives*, 31:1 (2017), 3–24.

Nye, J. S. 'The rise of China's soft power', *Wall Street Journal Asia* (29 December 2005).

Nye, J. S. 'Soft power: The origins and political progress of a concept', *Palgrave Communications*, 3 (2017), https://dx.doi.org/10.1057/palcomms.2017.8.

O'Brien, D. 'The mountains are high and the Emperor is far away: An examination of ethnic violence in Xinjiang', *International Journal of Chinese Studies*, 2:2 (2011), 389–406.

O'Brien, K. J. and Y. Deng. 'Preventing protest one person at a time: Psychological coercion and relational repression in China', *The China Review*, 17:2 (2017), 179–201.

Olesen, A. 'China reacts to massive corruption tally of a fallen general', *Foreign Policy* (22 November 2014), http://foreignpolicy.com/2014/11/22/china-reacts-to-massive-corruption-tally-of-a-fallen-general/ (last accessed 14 May 2018).

Palmer Kaup, K. *Creating the Zhuang: Ethnic Politics in China* (Boulder, CO: Lynne Rienner, 2000).

Pei, M. *China's Crony Capitalism* (Cambridge, MA: Harvard University Press, 2016).

Phillips, T. 'Chinese troops stage show of force in Xinjiang and vow to "relentlessly beat" separatists', *Guardian* (20 February 2017), www.theguardian.com/world/2017/feb/20/chinese-troops-stage-show-of-force-in-xinjiang-and-vow-to-relentlessly-beat-separatists.

Phillips, T. 'Chinese university puts CCTV in dormitories to encourage "good study habits"', *Guardian* (16 June 2016), www.theguardian.com/world/2016/jun/16/chinese-university-students-cctv-surveillance-wuchang (last accessed 14 May 2018).

Phillips, T. 'Ghost town: How China emptied Hangzhou to guarantee "perfect" G20', *Guardian* (5 September 2016), www.theguardian.com/world/2016/sep/05/ghost-town-how-china-emptied-hangzhou-to-guarantee-perfect-g20 (last accessed 14 May 2018).

Pieke, F. *The Good Communist: Elite Training and State Building in Today's China* (Cambridge: Cambridge University Press, 2009), 14–18.

Piketty, T., L. Yang and G. Zucman. 'Capital accumulation, private property and rising inequality in China, 1978–2015', *NBER Working Paper No. 23368* (Cambridge, MA: National Bureau of Economic Research, 2017).

Pooler, M. 'Chinese steel production to slow sharply in 2018', *Financial Times* (9 January 2018), www.ft.com/content/7dfb918e-f087–11e7-b220–857e26d1aca4 (last accessed 14 May 2018).

Pye, L. 'China: Erratic state, frustrated society', *Foreign Affairs*, 69:4 (1990), 56–74.

Ran, T. 'China's land grab is undermining grassroots democracy', *Guardian* (16 December 2011), www.theguardian.com/commentisfree/2011/dec/16/china-land-grab-undermining-democracy (last accessed 14 May 2018).

Rana, D. S. *The Current Chinese Defence Reforms and Impact on India* (New Delhi: Centre for Land Warfare Studies, 2017).

Richards, K. *China-India: An Analysis of the Himalayan Territorial Dispute* (Canberra: Centre for Defence and Strategic Studies, 2015).

Rong, M. 'A new perspective in guiding ethnic relations in the 21st century: "De-politicization" of ethnicity in China', *Asian Ethnicity*, 8:3 (2007), 199–217.

Schwartlander, B. 'Are we losing the war on pollution?', *China Daily* (6 January 2017), www.chinadaily.com.cn/china/2017–01/06/content_27881815.htm (last accessed 14 May 2018).

Shambaugh, D. 'China's soft-power push', *Foreign Affairs*, 95 (July/August 2015), 99–107.

Shen, X. and K. S. Tsai. 'Institutional adaptability in China: Local developmental models under changing economic conditions', *World Development*, 87 (2016), 107–27.

Statista. 'Migrant workers in China – statistics & facts' (31 May 2013), www.statista.com/topics/1540/migrant-workers-in-china/ (last accessed 14 May 2018).

Sun, W., X. Wang and Y. Zhou. 'How free do people feel to express their opinions? A study in urban China', *Applied Economics Letters*, 19:12 (2012), 1165–9.

Teets, T. 'The politics of policy innovation in China: Local officials as policy entrepreneurs', *Issues & Studies*, 51:2 (2016), 79–109.

Tong, Y. 'Morality, benevolence, and responsibility: Regime legitimacy in China from past to the present', *Journal of Chinese Political Science*, 16:2 (2011), 141–59.

Tsang, S. 'Consultative Leninism: China's new political framework', *Journal of Contemporary China*, 18:62 (2009), 865–80.

Tse, D. 'Why General Fang Fenghui was purged', *The Diplomat* (14 January 2018), https://thediplomat.com/2018/01/why-general-fang-fenghui-was-purged/ (last accessed 14 May 2018).

Wan, W. 'In China, one in five children live in villages without their parents', *Washington Post* (30 December 2013), www.washingtonpost.com/world/asia_pacific/in-china-one-in-five-children-live-in-rural-villages-without-their-parents/2013/12/30/3f05a870–4b9a-11e3–9890-a1e0997fb0c0_story.html (last accessed 14 May 2018).

Wang, J. 'Representations of the Chinese Communist Party's political ideologies in President Xi Jinping's discourse', *Discourse & Society*, 28:4 (2017), 413–35.

Wang, Q. 'China to "declare war" on pollution, cut energy use', *China Daily* (14 March 2014), www.chinadaily.com.cn/china/2014npcandcppcc/2014–03/14/content_17346330.htm (last accessed 14 May 2018).

Wike, R., J. Poushter, L. Silver and C. Bishop. 'Globally, more name U.S. than China as world's leading economic power', *Pew Research Center* (13 July 2017), www.pewglobal.org/2017/07/13/more-name-u-s-than-china-as-worlds-leading-economic-power/ (last accessed 14 May 2018).

Wildau, G. and T. Mitchell. 'China income inequality among world's worst', *Financial Times* (14 January 2016), www.ft.com/content/3c521faa-baa6–11e5-a7cc-280dfe875e28 (last accessed 14 May 2018).

Wu, X., D. L. Yang and L. Chen. 'The politics of quality-of-life issues: Food safety and political trust in China', *Journal of Contemporary China*, 26:106 (2017), 601–15.

Xinhua. 'Bo Xilai gets life in prison', *China Daily* (22 September 2013), http://usa.chinadaily.com.cn/china/2013–09/22/content_16984347.htm (last accessed 14 May 2018).

Xinhua. 'CPC has nearly 89.5 mln members', *China Daily* (30 June 2016), http://usa.chinadaily.com.cn/china/2017–06/30/content_29952372.htm (last accessed 14 May 2018).

Xinhua. 'Xi calls for strengthened ideological work in colleges', *China Radio International* (9 December 2016), http://english.cri.cn/12394/2016/12/09/3521s946891.htm (last accessed 14 May 2018).

Xinhua. 'Principal contradiction facing Chinese society has evolved in new era: Xi', *China Daily* (18 October 2017), www.chinadaily.com.cn/china/19thcpcnationalcongress/2017–10/18/content_33401026.htm (last accessed 14 May 2018).

Xinhua. 'Xi calls for furthering SOE reform', *China Daily* (18 October 2017), www.chinadaily.com.cn/china/2017–10/18/content_33403609.htm (last accessed 14 May 2018).

Xue, K., X. Chen and M. Yu. 'Can the World Expo change a city's image through foreign media reports?', *Public Relations Review*, 38:5 (2012), 746–54.

Yang, Y. 'Factbox: Seven facts of China's anti-corruption campaign', *Xinhua* (4 July 2017), http://news.xinhuanet.com/english/2017–07/04/c_136416939.htm (last accessed 14 May 2018).

Yang, Y. and Y. Yang. 'Smile to enter: China embraces facial-recognition technology', *Financial Times* (8 June 2017), www.ft.com/content/ae2ec0ac-4744–11e7–8519–9f94ee97d996 (last accessed 14 May 2018).

Yuan, Y. 'Soft power of international news media: American audiences' perceptions of China's country image mediated by trust in news' (Doctoral thesis, University of Maryland, 2017), https://drum.lib.umd.edu/handle/1903/19797 (last accessed 14 May 2018).

Zang, X. *Ethnicity in China: A Critical Introduction* (New York, NY: Wiley, 2015).

Zenz, A. and J. Leibold. 'Xinjiang's rapidly evolving security state', *China Brief*, 17:4 (2017), 21–7.

Zhang, X., M. S. Brown and D. O'Brien. '"No CCP, no New China": Discourses of pastoral powering the Xinjiang region of China', *China Quarterly* (Forthcoming, 2018).

Zhang, Y. 'Adapting Marxism called crucial', *China Daily* (30 September 2017), www.chinadaily.com.cn/china/2017–09/30/content_32668217.htm (last accessed 14 May 2018).

Zhao, X. 'Colleges vital for Party', *China Daily* (9 December 2016), www.chinadaily.com.cn/china/2016–12/09/content_27617484.htm (last accessed 14 May 2018).

Zhou, L. 'Trust crisis in US institutions as Chinese confidence rises, Edelman global poll finds', *South China Morning Post*

(22 January 2018), www.scmp.com/news/china/diplomacy-defence/article/2130081/trust-crisis-us-institutions-chinese-confidence-rises (last accessed 14 May 2018).

Zhou, S. and X. Yu. 'Regional heterogeneity of life satisfaction in urban China: Evidence from hierarchical ordered logit analysis', *Social Indicators Research*, 132:1 (2017), 25–45.

Index